The Longest Bridge across Water

The Longest Bridge across Water

An Ordinary Man's Encounters with an Unordinary God

BY JEREMY MANGERCHINE

Jeremy Mangerchine
P.O. Box 791072
New Orleans, LA 70179

ISBN: - 13: 978-1494303723

ISBN: - 10: 1494303728

Printed in the United States of America

Dedication

I dedicate this book to Shannon, the most blameless and upright person I know.

Shannon, when I had very little interest in knowing the heart of God, you were consistently meeting with Him. Your consistency and steadfastness are truly remarkable and have been the backbone of our beautiful family. You carry a gift of faith so profound, if I wasn't your husband, I would never believe it was real. Your purity of heart and ability to selflessly love and serve is humbling and inspiring.

You are an amazing mother and wife. Even more than that, you understand that you are God's beloved "Wildflower".

It is a tremendous honor to be your husband, and I cannot wait to see what God has in store for you as you continue to dream with Him. The impossible does not exist in your realm, and I am committed to backing you in anything that you are called to do.

I. Love. You.

Acknowledgements

Noah and Elisha, you boys are such a gift. I cannot wait to see what you become. I see glimpses of it already, and I cannot comprehend the half of it. I am confident that you will be far more grounded in your understanding and relationship with God, and at a far younger age than me. I long for the day when your eyes are opened and I can sit under your teaching and be blown away by Christ in you.

Thank you to Dad, Mom, Bryan and Lisa. You are each amazing people, and I am truly blessed and thankful to have you as my family.

Thank you to each and every one of you who we are proud to call friends. Thank you for your love and support, and for just being you. We love all of you deeply.

Contents

Foreword

I know Jeremy.

We've prayed together, planned together, traveled to India together, healed together, laughed together, worshipped together, and, together have been blown away by the intense intimacy and power of Christ in our lives.

Neither of us has any seminary training. Neither one of us is someone you would look at, outside of Christ, and gasp, "Oh My Gosh, what an amazing individual!" In the end, we're two ordinary guys, average Joes, or, as Jeremy likes to call us, "dumb hosers."

The difference is this: Christ introduced himself to me 36 years ago (today actually), whereas he became a living reality in Jeremy's life maybe three years ago. Where my life has been a long slow walk into the actual moment—by—moment experience of Christ's presence, Jeremy's has been like Alice tumbling down the rabbit hole or Dorothy being swept up in that Kansas cyclone. God has taught Jeremy awesome truths and showed him wondrous mysteries in an amazingly short period of time.

What I know is this: Jeremy's story is open to everyone. It's not exclusive, not a revelation of great spiritual truths only gained after years and years of intense dedication and discipline. It's God lavishing His love and truth, entering into a profound intimacy with an average Joe. Like me. And like you.

The door is open for you to enter into the same amazing world, the same rich relationship, the same spiritual wealth, the same confidence and peace.

Come on in.

Dave Diamond

Director & Founder of Faith and Freedom Ministries

Introduction

I'm a normal Christian guy. I spent most of my adult life as a businessman and entrepreneur. Though I grew up in the Church, in a ministry family, it was never really my thing. Don't get me wrong; I believed in God and half-heartedly tried to please and follow Him, despite Him seeming so distant. But I wasn't exactly passionate about it. If you had asked me why I was a Christian, I probably would not have known what to say—and I would have scrounged up something about how my parents raised me that way or my desire to avoid hell. And that about summed it up for me. As far as I could tell, the Christian life pretty much sucked, and I pretty much sucked at living up to the standards I had been told mattered.

At the same time, I always sensed the existence of something more—some mystical reality that must be far bigger, sweeter, and more wonderful than all the stuff I had ever been told. My heart whispered this to me, but I had never seen or heard of it in the lives of the Christians I knew. It did not at all connect with my daily reality, and because of that, it wasn't something I thought about much.

Then something funny happened. I started working a day job, and to get there, I had to drive over the longest bridge over water in the world—the Lake Pontchartrain Causeway. It is twenty-six miles long. Every day, back and forth I went for miles across water. My journey across this bridge is a lot like my journey into the Spirit. The Bible sometimes uses water as a metaphor for the Spirit. It is fluid and flexible; it gives and sustains life. In large quantities, it is so powerful that humans have a hard time harnessing it. And if we jump into it, we are engulfed. So it is with the Spirit.

It took me a few years, but eventually, during this season of driving across water, God began to stir my heart with His love and goodness. Slowly, I started to hope the *something* I had believed in might actually be possible. This book is the story of that journey across water, that simple drive into the things of the Spirit and the long and deep and wide heart of God. Along the way, I saw and experienced some pretty crazy stuff. Things I didn't even think possible. I'm sharing my story with you because I want you to know—just in case you don't—what's available. See, I didn't get to go on this journey because I'm somehow more special than the rest of God's kids.

We are all in a different place with Christ. Each one of us is on a different mile of the bridge into our discovery of His presence. But no matter where we are, we are qualified to encounter the living God. I am proof of that. So is Paul the apostle, the dude who ran around persecuting and murdering Christians before Jesus knocked him down and told him what's up. And Paul and I are also proof that Christianity is a lot more exciting than many of us have been taught.

Like I said, this book is about what's possible. It's the wild tale of an ordinary guy (me) who suddenly discovered the *something* tugging at his heart was not only real, but the most intoxicating and thrilling journey ever. This book comes with a promise and an invitation. The promise is that if it's possible for me, it's possible for you. If you've realized Jesus is your savior, you have the same God living inside you, and let's face it—nothing is impossible with Him. And that, of course, is the invitation. Consider yourself invited to experience the limitless goodness of God. Are you ready to go for the ride of your life? To drive out over the water and see what happens?

Then buckle up. It might be a little scary, but it will definitely be a lot of fun!

Chapter 1

Waking Up

Awake, my glory! Awake, harp and lyre! I will awaken the dawn. —Psalm 57:8

Staring at the journal in my hands, a black 200-page unlined sketch book, I paused to think. One word described that year for me: *stirring.*

When my wife, Shannon, and I had moved to New Orleans, I had started working a salaried, clock-in-and-clock-out, eight-to-five job for the first time in my adult life. Before that, I lived the life of an independent contractor, making my own schedule and building my own business, not working for the man and coordinating my life to his rules. It was not an easy adjustment. Even worse, my company's office was an hour drive from my home over that bridge I mentioned in the introduction, the longest bridge over water in the world, the Lake Pontchartrain Causeway.

The truth is I hated leaving my home before dark and getting home after dark and never having any time when I wasn't being told what to do. So I had started waking up at 5 a.m., making coffee, and wasting a bunch of time on the Internet before I left for work. I was accomplishing nothing of any substance or value, but, in my desire for independence, I felt compelled to do it. Afterward, I would make my drive across the bridge. And every morning, at first without knowing it, I had gotten closer and closer to *something,* a stirring and swirling in heart I couldn't yet explain.

It had started somewhere in the monotony between the spring and summer of that year. Suddenly, surprisingly, I had begun to sense God speaking to me. I had never had a conversational relationship with Him before, so I wasn't quite sure, but it seemed like that was what was happening. I felt Him saying He wanted those early morning hours to be for me and Him, promising that if I would give it to Him, He would do really cool stuff. I didn't really know what that meant, and I hadn't been willing to find out. Instead, I spent the better part of the year ignoring His invitation.

Eventually, fed up with the self-centeredness that I had empowered in my life, my lack of spiritual growth, and my self-inflicted guilt over not obeying the prompting of the Holy Spirit, I found myself staring at my journal and preparing to write something revolutionary.

Father,

I am sick and tired of being defined, guided and manipulated by self-centered desires. From the time I wake up until the time I close my eyes at night, I feel like I am obsessed with fulfilling my own needs, wants and desires. You have blessed me beyond belief with You, and a wife, and baby—blessed me beyond anything I ever dreamed I would have. Yet I do not see this because I am constantly blinded by my selfishness.

Jesus, I surrender it all to You and Your power! I cannot do life on my own! I need You. I am tired of running from You.

I surrender my pride to You, my fear to You, my insecurity to You, my ignorance to You, and my judgmentalism to You.

Use me as a vessel to lead those who do not know You toward laying down their lives at Your feet. Use me, God! Empower me to be a good steward.

For the next few months, I *tried* to walk out what I had written. I made a really solid effort. Through my efforts, I found a little success, but it was hardly profound. I had no idea what it meant to draw on the power of God in order to truly walk out this new life which I had committed myself to in my heart.

Regardless, something had changed inside me. Hunger began stirring deep in my spirit, and I could tell a process had begun. I didn't know what it was or what would happen, but I knew the awakening had already begun. Gradually, God began answering my prayer. At the time, I didn't grasp the magnitude of the shift He was working in my heart and life. The fact is, I needed a lot of purging, and God needed my cooperation. In His kindness, God acted very slowly.

Spiritual realities became increasingly intriguing to me in a way they never had been before. I knew so little about the power of God or spiritual realities—how I felt about them, how to operate in them, and whether they were really available to me. And for the first time, I found myself desperately hungry for the supernatural. I suddenly knew I couldn't settle for the world's counterfeits. I wanted the real, and I wanted to personally know the source, the one true Source.

Then in late December, as I was cleaning out my protein shake maker in the kitchen of the office at work, I struck up a conversation with a co-worker named Ken. He and I had chatted occasionally over the previous two years, but, even though I knew he was a brother in the Lord, I had never really connected with him.

As he was talking, the Holy Spirit whispered in my ear, "Get to know him, because I am going to use him to take you through the next phase of your walk with Me." His voice was as clear as day. I had no idea why the Lord had spoken so clearly or what the next phase was, but I knew I had to go for it. It didn't take long for me to discover Ken knew God in a way unlike anything I had ever seen. Over the next months, his friendship was pivotal in introducing me to that *something* I had always felt I was created for. I just hadn't known how to connect the dots. Ken did, and, through him, God lit the dynamite called my life.

One day, as we drove to lunch during our one-hour break, Ken casually asked me, "How do you hear God?"

Prior to that, I had always hidden behind a buffer of religious jargon to avoid having to reveal my true self. But Ken has a way of peering deep into people's eyes, seeming to read the deepest secrets of their souls. He also likes to ask the type of pointed questions that make me squirm. This was one such question. I thought for a moment, trying to figure out how to answer the question. I could only think of a few times when I believed God had clearly given me direction. I decided to give the best-sounding (and most cliché) answer I knew.

First, I told him I heard God through the Bible (though at that time I barely read it and hadn't actually had any major revelation from the Bible).

Second, I mentioned circumstances. What I didn't mention was that this type of hearing tended to be a shot in the dark for me because I hardly knew the heart of God, making my interpretations of any circumstance misguided at best.

Third, I listed the counsel of others, which sounds noble and good (and actually is, given its proper place), but, because I didn't hear God or know His heart very well, I could be easily swayed by the counsel of others. I gave their voices an inappropriate weightiness, making too many decisions and determining my beliefs and convictions based on their opinions and revelation.

All was about to change—drastically!

You see, if the word for that year was *stirring,* the word for the next year was *explosion!* It began one day as I was driving to work and listening to a teaching by a well-known prophet—until the King of kings and Lord of lords interrupted me. By that time, I had become a bit more aware of the voice of God, but I mostly just heard whispers here and there. At first, that was how He spoke to me in the car, quietly inviting me to turn off the teaching. I like to describe it as the voice of God that flows out of our spirits and permeates our inner ear. When I didn't comply, He got a lot louder.

To be fair, I was not at all used to this sort of thing. I wasn't intentionally ignoring Him; I just wasn't exactly sure what to do. And I certainly had no idea what was about to happen.

Suddenly, the presence of God swooped into my car from the right-hand side. It was intense and immense; the heaviness of His presence overwhelmed me. A very direct and firm voice, not from within, but externally, told me, "Turn off the sermon. Now!"

Clearly, He wanted my complete and full attention. He then told me I was going to begin to hear Him in ways to which I was not accustomed, and He promised to teach me many things. He told me it was imperative I learned how to rest.

"Rest?" I asked, "Like a vacation?"

"I will show you," He said. And that was that.

Within just a few months, rest did indeed become the place from which I live, and it enabled me to hear Him and to release His love and power.

When God spoke to me that day in my car, He initiated the turning point of my life that led to the wild journey of discovery in the Spirit which this book chronicles. Everything leading up to that moment was a wooing, an invitation, a stirring. But when the one true God visited me in such an undeniable way, clearly letting me know His good intentions for me and what I was supposed to do, I was ruined for anything else. This became my reference point for who God is and His desire to reveal Himself to me. My lens for viewing God and the entire world had, in a moment, been broken and reshaped. All I knew was that I needed to know and experience more. I was hooked.

It's a good thing, too, because over the years I had acquired quite the concoction of religious and fear-induced garbage that kept me bound by my pride and prevented me from expressing my heart to God. For years, even when I'd felt the urge to express my heart in worship, pride and fear of man would begin whispering to me: *If you raise your hands, you will look stupid. You don't really want to do that do you? You don't want to look stupid.* And I believed them—then. Now that I had tasted the goodness of God's love for me and *heard* His voice, I was obsessed with experiencing Him. Pride can't compete with that.

That year, New Year's Day fell on a Sunday, and I felt the Holy Spirit leading me to fast. As far as I was concerned, God could have told me to do *anything* and I would have done it. It was my first fast ever, and I faced it with eagerness and determination and a heart of desire. The church we were attending took a break over the holidays, so there were no services to attend. Both Shannon and I wanted to find somewhere to worship, so we and another couple from another church decided to visit the Vineyard church in the suburbs.

I had a very good opinion of the Vineyard movement, as I had sporadically attended one of the main churches in Columbus, Ohio, while in high school. Several years later, I had attended and played guitar at a smaller Vineyard church in Myrtle Beach. I thoroughly enjoyed that church, and I remember feeling the presence of God there in a way I hadn't before. Now I was again attending a Vineyard, only everything was different. I was different. I was ready to encounter God and to be catapulted into a new reality in Him. I didn't know what it would look like; I just knew I wanted it.

The music that day was surprisingly bad in terms of quality and skill, but what the band lacked in ability, the Holy Spirit more than made up for in anointing. The presence of God was thick, and more and more I could feel myself falling under the influence of the Holy Spirit. The urge to let go of all my inhibitions and let loose and worship bubbled up strongly within me. I so badly wanted to let my hands shoot up toward Heaven. Slowly, I pulled my hands out of my pockets and began to raise them.

Letting go was amazing!

As I did, something broke in me. Something changed. It wasn't in the outward act of raising my hands; it was in my heart. Pride, self-consciousness and fear hung their heads as I relinquished control and let myself fall into the arms of God. I began to melt into the warmth of His embrace, where the fear of people has no say. That fear had kept its claws in me for so long, preventing me from living out my identity as a worshiper. But in the embrace of my Father, I stepped past fear and into the river of His presence.

Not surprisingly, it wasn't long after my experience at the Vineyard that I began speaking in tongues. For me, that was a really big deal. Just imagine, if lifting my hands in worship freaked me out, what the prospect of speaking in tongues might do to me! The thought created only fear and skepticism in me, and I wanted no part of it. However, as God began to stir my heart toward Him, my attitude toward tongues began to shift as well. So I prayed a silly prayer that went like this, "God, if You want me to speak in tongues, make me do it."

In response, the Holy Spirit began showing me how wrong my perspective on tongues was. While He does sometimes overwhelm people in such a way that they begin to speak in tongues without warning, it is like any other gift from Him, and we learn to cooperate with Him and release it from our vessel.

When I finally did begin praying in tongues, I still had little understanding of the mysterious language. One day, while I sat and talked with God, I decided the best thing to do would be to go to the source and ask Him about it. I did not at all expect what I heard. The fact is, I didn't know I would be learning a new language that would become a vital means of communication between my spirit and the Spirit of the living God.

God responded to my question by pulling me into a vision. Scrolling across my view were words written in a strange language I had never before seen. Like a ticker tape from right to left, they appeared and disappeared. Though I couldn't naturally read them, when the words appeared, my spirit recognized them and was able to read them. As I read the words, I also then spoke them. These words were not from any human language, but a spiritual language the Spirit of God wanted to personally teach me. The language I learned in that vision is not what I speak constantly. Sometimes I mutter it under my breath, and when I am in public, I speak it in my spirit. This language communicates my inner most feelings, thoughts, and desires directly to the Spirit of God within me, most of which I am unaware.

Truly, this is an incredible gift. Yet even after I began to speak in tongues, pride and self-consciousness kept me from flowing freely in it at first. Every time I began to speak out loud the words I felt in my heart, my mind would hear and perceive them as foolishness, and I would immediately feel self-conscious, shutting down the flow on the spot. Determined to break through this self-imposed barrier, I took the opportunity to pray in the Spirit every time I was alone. While I saw some improvement, it was not to the extent I had hoped for.

Then, one day I was riding in the car with a person of great influence in my life, and I felt strongly that I needed to share this new experience with him. Nervously, I cleared my throat. As fairly conservative people, speaking in tongues was not a common topic of conversation, and I assumed he would frown upon my wonderful new treasure. I was wrong. When I finally gathered the courage to spit out my news, he said matter-of-factly, "I've been speaking in tongues since 1974."

What in the world!? I thought, smiling with amazement. Suddenly, I felt a new freedom in my heart, and all the self-imposed self-consciousness lifted. Since then, my prayer language has developed amazingly and has proven to be one of the most intimate, edifying, faith-building aspects of my spiritual life. The truth is, I love it. And amazingly, it was only the beginning of my incredible journey into the Spirit.

The Longest Bridge across Water

Chapter 2

The Roar of His Voice

The voice of the LORD makes the deer to calve and strips the forests bare; and in His temple everything says, "Glory!" —Psalm 29:9

It was 4 a.m. I had a quiet house and two full cups of coffee steaming next to me—a perfect recipe for a fun time with my best friend. During the silence of the early mornings while the city enjoyed its sleep, I discovered a life-altering treasure. I began to encounter God in ways I didn't know were even possible. Quite literally, I had no grid for what He had begun to show me. It didn't take long for those sacred times to become my favorite thing to do in the entire world. While I sipped my coffee, my Father sat and talked with me. I had begun to hear His voice regularly and often, but the mornings were unique. He spoke so loudly and with such clarity that it really was like conversing with Him as He sat on the sofa next to me.

One morning, He started telling me about His voice and how He talks to people. All of the sudden, He appeared in front of me in an open vision (when your eyes are open and an image appears before you). I saw a square frame like a television screen, with His face smack dab in the center of it, except His person was only light. It looked like a box on a website where there is supposed to be a picture, but the picture is not there yet. It was just a blank frame from the chest to the top of the head.

"Jeremy," He said, "people need to understand that I am always talking."

I knew He talked often, and all people have the ability to hear Him, but I never considered that He might be *always* talking.

"Yeah, watch this," He said. Immediately, He started saying over and over and over again, "I'm talking, I'm talking, I'm talking, I'm talking..." And as He repeated those words, His voice was crystal clear, and nothing was drowning it out.

Picture a window frame with a head, from the shoulders up. In the area around His outline, there was nothingness. Then, as if a curtain was being rolled upward, images began filling the surface area around His outline from the bottom up, things like cars, trees, buildings, roads—basically city life. All the while, He was repeating, "I'm still talking, I'm still talking, I'm still talking..."

The images came with sound, too. As they scrolled up the screen from bottom to top, the corresponding sounds of cars driving by, birds chirping, and so forth also increased. Still, He kept saying, "I'm still talking, I'm still talking, I'm still talking..." But as the pictures moved higher and the sounds grew louder, His voice became fainter, drowned out more and more by the additional noise, until it was completely indistinguishable.

Then the reverse happened. The images began descending on the screen, and their noises began decreasing in volume. As they did, gradually, in proportion to the fading of the other noises, the voice of God increased in volume. And there He was: "I'm still talking, I'm still talking, I'm still talking..."

Once it was only Him again, He said, "See, I'm always talking. You just need to learn to tune into My voice in the midst of loud, chaotic lives."

"I never want to let Your voice be tuned out," I said. I was determined to maintain this closeness and dialogue the entire day. However, by the time I got ready for work, got out of the house and into my car, and was headed for work, I was nearly completely tuned out.

Hearing the voice of God is a lifestyle that is practiced and cultivated over time. I obviously still had some growing to do. This began a season in which God taught me a great deal about how to hear Him and how to deal with the things that so often crowd out His voice in our daily lives. This is something He desires to do for each of His children, to walk us through the process of learning what His voice sounds like and how to decipher it from the noise and endless stimuli of our modern world.

Here's a bit of what He taught me.

How *Not* to Hear

One of the first misconceptions about the voice of God that had to go was my tendency to try really hard to hear Him.

Through most of my life, I usually only approached God with a question when I faced something urgent. I felt like I really, really needed to hear Him say something *right now!* "Do I take this job offer? Do I go to this school? Do I propose to my girlfriend?" But by the time my question had become urgent enough that I asked God about it, I would have very little peace as I anxiously awaited an answer from on high. As I'm sure you can guess, it didn't work so well that way. Not only would I be too stressed and too out of practice in conversing with Him to actually discern His voice in the midst of the noise, but it was also less than ideal relational dynamics. After all, it is weird and not very complementary to have a relationship with someone, let alone my eternal Father, only when I want or need something. This is especially true since He had been pursuing me and talking to me all along (and I had been, for the most part, ignoring Him).

Thankfully, He is really patient and doesn't hold it against us when we do this. He really does have our best interest in mind and wants us to know His voice. What He showed me is that I am always listening to something. Often, it's just not Him. Even the worry related to needing direction from Him or the guilty feelings about not listening to Him become noise that blocks Him out. I learned I just needed to chill out and take it easy. He is not stressed, and I shouldn't be either.

One time the Holy Spirit said to me, "I talk to you more than you talk to Me. I'm just a better listener." Ouch.

At times I am a good listener; at other times, not so much. One of the greatest benefits I've found in journaling my development with the Lord is the ability it gives me to look back and see when I've have been a poor listener in my relationship with God. For example, I would ask Him something one day and then switch to another thing the next day, not realizing He was in the process of answering my previous question. I look back with the benefit of hindsight and see how idiotic I was, but the truth is, it was accidental. It is a growth process.

We all have the ability to discern whether a person is actually listening to us when we talk. God is even better at that than we are. It is so easy to say we want to hear God and even to ask Him a question, but often the idea of treating Him with the respect we would give to another person hardly crosses our minds. If while I am having a conversation with Shannon, I frequently look at my phone or am off in la-la land, I am communicating to her that I don't really want to hear what she has to say. The same is true in my relationship with God.

Inner Silence

The second lesson I learned related to the amount of inner chaos in my life and what it means to really rest. Rest is a place every human desperately wants to visit. This place is safe, free of stress and uncertainty, removed from the pull of anxieties and agendas. It is soft and calm. The prevailing mindset regarding how one attains this blissful state of rest goes something like this: if I work hard enough, I can justify resting for a week or two, get away to my favorite vacation spot, and escape all my worries. Rest will finally be attained and will hopefully carry me over through the following year.

The Holy Spirit told me, "Many people retreat to find rest, only to vacation just outside the door to rest."

This idea changed my life. My inner chaos had acquired for me a prescription for hypertension medication since the age of seventeen. I was reactionary in every sense of the word. And my constant internal chaos kept me from truly connecting with God. Think about it. If your emotions and mind are swirling and always chasing after a million things, it is impossible to focus on or connect with anyone, let alone a God you can't see with your natural eyes. The answer is rest, which fortunately is a place we all want to live in anyway. Simply put, it is living from the reality of Christ's summing up of all things on the cross. Through revelation knowledge of this truth, we are able to truly live freely, divorced from self-effort and relying completely on the power of the life of God that flows out of us.

The first step in my journey toward rest was to deal with what God had shown me to be the largest cause of blockage in my ability to hear His voice—inner chaos. In a loud and busy world, stress and anxiety can easily become the loudest voices screaming in our heads. That looks different for everyone, and there are many self-imposed causes for inner chaos, but for me, the biggest cause was my use of technology. I'm pretty sure a lot of people can relate to me on this one, too.

Technology itself is morally neutral. It is a wonderful tool that can be used for good or bad purposes. It can be managed, or it can manage us. I love and enjoy using many of the improvements of modern technology. But like anything else that is good and enjoyable, it can become addictive. For me, it certainly was.

It all started with TV. From a young age, I was hooked. My parents did a great job moderating my intake, though I attempted to push the boundaries as far as possible. When I left for college and could fall asleep with the TV on and never turn it off, I was pumped. I could endlessly feed my addiction without any accountability. What I didn't realize was that I had created a relationship with technology. And I loved it very much.

I was absolutely unaware of my addiction to chaos. I didn't know why silence freaked me out. The eeriness of being by myself, with just my thoughts and a quiet room, was enough to make me twitch—literally. As a technology junkie, I desperately needed the buzz of something electrical humming my way. (And I know I'm not alone in this!) Like so many others, I would wake up in the morning and immediately and compulsively need to check Facebook, Twitter, my email, and whatever else before I even got out of bed. Once my feet hit the floor, the next step was turning on the TV so I could make breakfast while surrounded by the comfortable hum of technology.

As I mentioned at the beginning of Chapter 1, the time between when I woke up and left the house was consumed with compulsive social media and other random Internet activity. And thanks to my smart phone, this didn't have to stop just because I was driving. The same was true when I returned home.

Without realizing it, in a very real sense technology had become my Holy Spirit. Rather than resting in the timeless and unchanging God and learning to renew my mind to operate with the mind of Christ, I was changing with the world and allowing my brain to be rewired by the things of this world as communicated through technology.

When I first discovered my addiction to technology, I tried various formulas to discipline myself into freedom. It didn't work. It didn't matter how many times I resolved not to turn on the TV or look at my phone for an hour while I read my Bible and prayed. If addiction could be broken so simply, it wouldn't be addiction. And God was not impressed with my efforts. Later I realized He wasn't interested in me squeezing Him into my life. He didn't want a time slot; He wanted to be MY EVERYTHING.

Thankfully, He was (and is) very interested in meeting with me in a very real way, even in the midst of my chaos. And through His patient pursuit of meeting with me, eventually I discovered He offers a better version of what I subconsciously thought I needed from technology. He wanted all of me, but He didn't invade my party; instead, He politely and relentlessly invited me into His. He wasn't too concerned about my dysfunctional framework—actually, He had already fixed it on the cross—and He was inviting me into that reality. I love how He works.

I always considered myself a pretty chill person, but internally I was all over the place, and mass confusion was my only constant. I didn't even realize it until I tried to sit still in silence for twenty minutes.

God had told me I needed to learn how to rest; step one was to develop a baseline, an experience of silence and stillness, for my relationship with God. Like many people, I couldn't remember a time when I had actually experienced silence and my soul was not filled with a tangled mess of jumbled thoughts and feelings. Even when I tried to get quiet, those thoughts, feelings, and emotions started to confuse me at first, and it bothered me almost to the point of physical agitation. As I persisted, they became even louder, and I started to distinguish certain thoughts I hadn't even realized were there.

Through this process, God kept telling me, "Don't quit!" When the bombardment would hit me, I wouldn't flinch. I wouldn't allow myself to be distracted, but instead took the opportunity to ask the Spirit of grace to renew my mind and wipe out the distracting and chaotic thoughts warring against me and my awareness of God. I focused on my fullness and His glory which abundantly dwells within me. I asked the Spirit of God to fill every fiber of me, to invade and take control of me. This was how I learned to rest. To just relax and enjoy Him. As I did, I became increasingly aware of Him, and His peace and joy swept over me and overwhelmed me with His warmth and goodness.

Eventually, as I did this over and over again, I began to reach a place in my spirit where I felt so full of God that I wondered whether I had left planet Earth. In that awareness of God and my fullness in Him, the things I thought were so important, the things I had been planning to talk to Him about, no longer mattered to me at all. Over and over again, I became so enveloped in His overwhelming embrace and the rapture of His presence that I could do nothing but be. And in that place, I began to hear His voice for the first time in a way that left me saying, "Aha! How did I miss this all along?"

I began to discover how wonderful it is that our Father has invited us into His fellowship with Himself and has withheld nothing from us. I found He is very interested in our discovery of this wonderful truth of His generosity and forethought about us. And our inclusion in the perfect communion of the Father, Son, and Spirit was His purpose for us all along. He met me along my journey to pull me into His reality and show me not only what He has already done, but who I really am, and how He wants to use me to relate His will to the world.

He wants to do this for you, too. The communion of the Father, Son, and Spirit is a cosmic party, a delightful dance of peace and unity which we are invited to attend. As we do, we will continually grow in our understanding of the meaning of this wonderful mystery. He talks to us because He enjoys us and wants to spend eternity with us. Because of the desire of His heart for us, He has eternally bound Himself to us and made us one with Him. When we understand that, the only question that makes sense on this topic is, "Why the heck wouldn't He talk to us?"

The Longest Bridge across Water

Chapter 3

So This Is Living

To know the love of Christ which surpasses knowledge, that you may be filled up to all the fullness of God. —Ephesians 3:19

The best way I can describe what had begun happening to me is to say I felt like an airplane pilot sitting in the cockpit of an airplane with the power turned off. Then suddenly the power switched on, the sound of the engine began to rise, and all the lights of the controls within the cockpit where I sat flashed on. I was ready to fly.

At the cross, God made full provision for us to be able to freely experience Him and His heart without measure, and we don't have to jump through any hoops do to it. Once I tasted this reality, I was wrecked for anything else! I couldn't wait to get up in the morning, get on my knees, and speak to God. I was so eager to just be with Him, to see what He had in store for that morning. Finally, I had found something real. Not just a belief system or a bunch of witty, impressive-sounding ideas. No, I was getting to know the actual person who spoke the universe into existence. All my words fail to express the magnitude of this reality growing in my heart.

Getting up at 5 a.m. no longer gave me enough time to explore all God had for me each day. So I started waking up an hour earlier. I would first get on my knees and just talk to God. I would thank Him for all kinds of things and tell Him all I wanted to do was meet with Him, talk to Him, spend time with Him. I would invite Him into the room and the house. I would ask Holy Spirit to rise up from within me and permeate my soul, my flesh, my entire person. He was my new obsession, and He was all I wanted. He knew my heart and recognized my hunger for Him, and His response was to make Himself known to me, to allow me free access to His heart and mind.

We were becoming the best of friends.

Then one day someone recommended the book, *Diary of a Modern Mystic,* to me. I found it available online for free. For me, the term *mystic* had always carried with it a truckload of pre-conceived notions and fear. I associated *mystic* primarily with eastern mysticism and the New Age, which I wanted to stay far away from. I did not want to drift off into an exclusively experience-centered connection with the spirit realm through any means other than the blood of Jesus. As a result, I feared mystical experiences, thinking, *No way can visions, dreams, and trances be of God, can they?*

But because it had been highly recommended to me, I hesitantly read *Diary of a Modern Mystic.* To my surprise, it was a very short collection of letters and brief journal entries from a man who was a foreign missionary and who was absolutely obsessed with one thing—being connected to God all day every day. As I started to read, I wondered when the weird mystical parts would come that would make me feel awkward and offended. It never happened. This man's experiences were not weird at all; they were just rooted in a pure desire for every waking moment to be filled with awe at the oneness he shared with God. This simple, very brief book became a catalyst that challenged the way I approached God.

Redefining Discipline

It all started with my view of discipline. Because I believed effort invested into training and discipline are what causes desired results, it was easy for me to think that way in my walk with God. But God began to show me the truth that spiritual discipline is not at all about getting God to do something for me. I discovered I could not earn anything from Him that He had not already freely made available to me through Christ. God's definition of discipline is training ourselves to take authority over our thought lives and silence the inner chaos so we can be led by the Spirit. This is very different from how many Christians define discipline. As I wrestled with this reality, God helped me understand that the minds of supernatural new creations (Christians) need regular renewal to the reality of who we are and our oneness with Him. That is the essence of spiritual discipline.

This paradigm shift enabled me to see that individuals with healthy spiritual discipline aren't legalistic; they know regimen has no impact upon God's perception of them. However, developing a lifestyle of practicing the awareness of the presence of God and fellowship with Him can be a very beneficial and life-altering thing. To some people, this may seem ritualistic. It all depends on the motive. For me, I was driven by passion. My passion drove me to a regular meeting time with my Father.

My brain is usually random and all over the place. To prevent myself from being a complete flake, I need to maintain some routines in my life. For example, I try to get up and go to bed around the same time every day. I eat and go to the gym regularly around the same time as well. In some ways, I started to apply this same mentality to my walk with God. I set aside certain times throughout each day to meet with God. These started out as markers for a very busy life. And they were great times of connection and affection with the heart of the Father. At that point, I still worked in the corporate world, and I would sneak away for five minutes, hiding out in the nursing mothers' room at work to talk to God.

As our relationship progressed and I became more aware of Him, I began talking to Him between the marker times, to the point that those markers became almost unnecessary. I do still keep regular times with God now, not as a ritual but in order to protect something very special to me that, in the midst of a busy life, could easily get bumped out.

The truth is, very few humans become great in anything without discipline. The same applies to believers training their senses to be aware of God, His voice, and what He is up too. However, not only is God not limited to our little one-hour times with Him, nor is carving out those times what compels Him to meet with us. I have discovered that if I am truly meeting with Him, He will let me know if I become ritualistic, and He will lead me out of it.

Getting to Know Him

As I spent more and more time with Him, the once far-off God I had known about was quickly becoming much more than an idea. He had already become more tangible than any other person I knew. In some ways, He was exactly like I had heard Him described; in other ways, He was very different. He was better than I had ever imagined. Sometimes He talked to me with the gentle sternness of a loving father. At other times, He was easygoing and lighthearted. He even used humor on occasion. One time in particular, while I was talking to Him, He took me into a vision in which I was sitting on the lap of God the Father. Words weren't necessary. As I sat there, He leaned over to

His right side where Jesus was sitting, reached out, and caught Jesus off guard with a gentle but playful tug to His beard. Joyous laughter ensued. The Father then looked at me and said, "Do you see what we do? We just be."

Moments like these were what I lived for. All I wanted was to know God's perspective. I longed to hear Him, to sense Him, to have Him teach me. Sometimes He wanted to teach me. At other times, He had something for me to do. Eventually it hit home with me that His favorite thing was when He and I just enjoyed one another. From that place of communion with Him, He would invite me to do things with Him, teaching me to grow in my perspective from a slave mindset into the fullness of a son. I was truly getting to know the Father, not just learning to know *about* Him, and I loved it. I loved Him.

One morning, as I was reading the Book of Samuel, God interrupted me. I had never heard of God interrupting the reading of Scripture. He began to speak in a tone that sounded very snobbish.

"What are You doing?" I asked.

"That is how you are reading the Bible," He responded. Holy Spirit school is great, but it is also very humbling.

I could not do anything to earn an experience from God, but the truth is, He knew better than I did when I genuinely desired to know Him and commune with Him. His response to that desire was to open me up and allow me to understand Him. I would feel His feelings, think His thoughts, and know things I had no way of knowing. I would see things He saw. Everything was a means of communication from Him. The flock of seagulls that I observed chaotically conducting their business while I pumped gas contained a lesson. My life circumstances, whether good or bad, were constantly being turned into teaching opportunities. His voice became clearer as well as broader, and as He started to open the eyes of my spirit, I began to see visions.

He was always near and always Him. He felt emotions, but not in a frantic human sense. He was unchanging. When He showed me a vision of a night sky with a building that had smoke billowing out of it and allowed me to feel what He felt about what was happening (the burning of several hundred women and children in Syria), He wasn't erratic. He cared. It broke His heart that His children were being slaughtered. Why did He show me this? I believe He did it simply because I asked about what He cares about.

And then something really crazy started happening. At times as I was praying, God would grab my hand and pull me up past the outer atmosphere into space. He would have me look down at Earth and challenge me to think and see things from above, to zoom out of my segmented and narrow-minded view of life and the world that only includes my experiences, circumstances, and opinions. He would tell me to view the world and its events, not based on how my life would be affected but through His eyes. The more time I spent in awareness of His presence, communicating and learning from Him, the more my life underwent drastic transformation. The experiences created a tangible change in the way I interacted with the world around me.

One time as my wife, Shannon, and I were in the midst of an argument, I had to run to the grocery store to pick something up. As I walked through the front of the store, griping to myself about my argument with Shannon, God tapped me on the shoulder and said, "Buy her flowers, Jeremy." It wasn't a suggestion.

"I don't want to buy her flowers," I said.

He didn't respond. He didn't need to. His silence further drove home the point. I was being schooled by God

Himself, and He used exercises such as that to break down my pride and refine my character. I am still a work in progress, but I am a totally different person than I was in when it all began. A person cannot spend that much time with God and not begin to look like Him. It wouldn't be long before He would begin telling me to prophesy over and heal people at the grocery store (and other places, too).

What Was Missing?

Throughout this initial season of building relationship with my Father, one question kept running through my head. *How did I not know about this? Why did no one tell me?* What I was experiencing was so amazingly beyond anything I had imagined possible. I wondered why, growing up in the Church, I had never heard about this. Perhaps people had tried to tell me and I just wasn't listening. Had my heart been too hard to receive it before, or were the people I knew just as unaware as I had been? Either way, the seeds these people and the Holy Spirit had planted in my life had finally taken root and begun to grow.

As I mentioned in Chapter 1, I had always sensed I was created to be a part of something big—that intangible *something* that tugged at my heart even while I was far away from God in my mind. This belief wasn't arrogance or pride but a deep yearning in my soul to enter into the fullness of the destiny into which God had called me before the beginning of time.

Not long ago, my mom told me that even as a kid, I was always dissatisfied with ordinary Christianity as it was presented to me. But for years, I buried that discontent and settled for a fear—based, hell—avoidance mentality in relation to God. For example, I thought I had to pray every night before bed in order to confess my sins to God, ask forgiveness, and ask Him to come into my heart so I could be saved from hell and get to Heaven.

Where this idea of God came from, I am not quite sure, but, as I aged, it created a problem. You see, I am a very rational person, and I wasn't aware of my inherent right and ability to hear God and to connect with His heart, not to mention my individual gifting. Yet I had a deep longing and need for someone to understand me. I didn't know anyone who could understand the depths of me. I felt very alone. Though I believed God was real and had created the world and died on the cross to save me from my sins, I didn't know that infinite realms of glory were available to me. I didn't know I could fall into His presence and experience His peace, joy, hope, rest, and love. I had no idea He wanted to talk to me, that He is actually *eager* to speak with me and pursue my heart. Because I so desired someone to understand me but didn't know the only one who could, time and time again I latched onto people to try to meet this need. As you can probably imagine, this didn't work out well for me.

This loneliness and misunderstanding about who God is and what He wants from me created massive confusion and frustration in me. As a child and teenager, I would cry out to God and try to white knuckle my way through sin management in order to please Him, but to no avail. In hindsight, I see He was there, answering me the entire time; I just wasn't listening to His response. What I did hear didn't suit my liking, so I didn't comply. That was a key part of the problem. To me, God seemed distant and primarily concerned with obedience and good behavior. God didn't *seem* to care about my cries for help, but the truth is, He did. I didn't know He was after my heart.

All this led me to start smoking any kind of cigarette I could find in fifth grade. I turned to alcohol in sixth grade and pot in seventh. While standing stoned in a friend's driveway, sometime during my high school years, I told my friend that one day I would get my act together and start following God.

As you know, eventually I did, but it wasn't to start following His behavior modification or sin management programs. It was in response to His loving embrace—which I had finally felt. What I have experienced in God's presence makes sin look so unappealing. At last, I had found the source of fulfillment, and I was pursuing Him recklessly. At last I had been found by the one who knows me fully and perfectly, and in the joy and passion of relationship with Him, I found the freedom to live like He'd created me to be. At last I had set out on my journey into the Spirit and the huge heart of my Father.

The Longest Bridge across Water

Chapter 4

Schooled by the Holy Spirit

The Holy Spirit, whom the Father will send in My
name, He will teach you all things, and bring to
your remembrance all that I said to you.
—John 14:26

Toward the beginning of my awakening, the Lord appeared before me as a teacher in front of a class. He wrote on a board with different colored squiggly lines flowing out of His writing hand. As He wrote, He declared to me that I would begin to have what He referred to as "variable experiences."

What I learned, as my journey continued, was that I was in school—Holy Spirit school. I was being trained to walk not only in obedience but also in freedom and power. This training would occur in many different ways and include many out-of-my-comfort-zone experiences. He told me I would begin to hear Him in ways I was not used to. And He was right. I had no idea what I was in for. The next leg of my journey into the Spirit was about to get weird—and extremely fun!

Eyes to See

As my hunger for Scripture rapidly increased, I began reading with a new vigor. One morning, I read this verse:

Son of man, you live in the midst of a rebellious house, who have eyes to see but do not see, ears to hear, but do not hear, for they are a rebellious house (Ezekiel 12:2).

As soon as I read it, the Holy Spirit told me, "You have eyes and ears, but you aren't seeing or hearing."

"Lord," I said, "give me eyes to see and ears to hear. Open my eyes and ears. I want to see You and hear You."

A few mornings later, as I was praying in tongues with my eyes closed, images began to appear before me. Apparently, He had given me eyes to see! This was new for me, something I hadn't expected at all. I didn't know anyone who had experienced visions. It would be an understatement to say I was excited. *Will they continue to happen?* I wondered. *Will they increase? What in the world am I seeing anyway?*

For the first few days, the visions I saw were very random, and I didn't get any interpretations. But I wasn't concerned. I just felt amazed by the love and grace of God and the fact that He is so creative that He can communicate with me in such an unexpected way. As the days passed, the visions increased in frequency.

One morning, I saw a series of visions, all unique but related. And over the next few weeks, each of the visions I had seen came to pass. This was a new development. I sensed purpose, that God was opening something up in me for a specific reason. I felt excited!

Over time, the visions I saw during my prayer times continued to expand and evolve. Also, I began seeing visions sometimes when I laid down at night. As I would close my eyes, rather than seeing black nothingness, I would see images unfold in front of me. Usually they seemed random, and I hadn't been praying or seeking them in any way. I was actually caught off guard—in a good way. Once again God was increasing my sensitivity and ability to see. Nowadays, when I close my eyes, it's like I am watching TV, with moving images rather than still pictures, and there is even sound included. These visions are a language that the Lord has developed with me. He uses them communicate to me.

The truth is, God sometimes does some really trippy things. His realm, which He enables us to see with our spiritual eyes, is far more wacky than many of us realize. His normal is not our normal, and the quicker we realize and accept this (letting Him be God and letting His reality become ours), the more He will be able to show us.

Step Outside, Please

One of my beliefs that did not fit into God's realm was the idea that God does everything for a clear purpose. It sounds good. And we sure would like it if He always made perfect sense and did things according to how we would do them. One thing is for certain; His ways do not always make sense to us. Often He requires action on our part to make sure we are ready for what He is about to do.

The Holy Spirit revealed this to me during a vision I had while fellowshipping with the Lord. I was sitting in my "special spot." It was at the far end of the sofa in the corner of the room. I sat there every morning, and, through encountering God in such profound ways on a regular basis in that particular spot, I had formed an attachment to it.

Abruptly, I saw a vision very different from any other I had seen. I saw an ovular-shaped hole cut out of the corner opposite where I sat in that windowless room, and I could see through the house. It was very early in the morning, and, from my special spot on the sofa, I could see through the solid wall into the dark street lined with houses. Over the houses, I could see the lights of the hotels just about a

51

mile away in the French Quarter. It was like the substance of the walls in that spot simply vanished.

As I sat and looked with surprise, wondering what in the world was happening, the Lord answered my thought by asking me to go outside. After hesitating for a few long moments, I figured it would be wise to take Him up on His invitation.

I got up and walked across the room, wondering why I was being invited outside. *Am I going to be given some amazing revelation? Am I going to be visited by Jesus?*

I stepped through the door into the dark early morning stillness. Everything was exactly as it looked from the inside of the house through the hole in the walls. It was still, quiet, and a tad chilly by New Orleans standards. I waited for several moments, observing my surroundings. I remember the brisk air so clearly, and I could see the stars in the sky, a rare site from where our house was situated.

Then God spoke. What He said was not what I was expecting. At the moment, it did not seem profound, but since, I have learned it was one of many steps in His divine customized training process that He was walking me through. He simply said, "I wanted to see whether, if I called you out here, you would come out."

That was it! Encounter over.

It is so wonderful yet challenging to have a God who wants to walk us through what it looks like to walk with Him. What I was beginning to learn was that He is very interested in being the one to teach us what that means.

Little did I know that this was part of my preparation for what was to follow.

Blown Away

One day during my lunch break at work, God asked me something crazy. And I mean really, really crazy. But I guess that's the definition of *miracle,* isn't it? Something so ridiculous and beyond our human understanding or ability that it seems just plain crazy, something we could hardly believe without seeing it with our own eyes. God is the God of crazy miracles. He did them in the Bible, and He does them today, too.

This particular day, God asked me to skip my usual lunch break work out to take a walk with Him. It was hard for me to give up my work out because I really love it, but, after attempting some negotiation with God, I eventually gave in. Walking out of the office, I began my stroll down the back streets without knowing what I was doing or where I was going. As we walked, He guided my way.

Eventually, after a ten minute walk, He led me to a small, isolated park with a gazebo by a river, and there He told me to have a seat. I sat for a few minutes, watching ants march by on the ground, and I started to complain in my mind about the fact that it was very hot and humid out and there was absolutely no breeze to cool me off.

That's when God asked me His crazy question: "Do you want to command the wind?"

"Huh???" I said, shocked at what I had heard.

"Go ahead," He said.

I was not expecting that at all. But I was definitely going to give it a shot. Without hesitation, I said in a stern but quiet tone, "Wind, blow."

I didn't really expect anything to happen and wondered whether there was some underlying lesson that would be revealed through this activity. But then, just a few seconds after I spoke, a strong wind came from a distance and blew past me, causing previously dead still tree limbs to sway considerably and leaves to blow.

I could hardly believe what was happening. But it was very real, and I was very in awe.

Then God said, "Tell the wind to stop." Maybe He wanted to show me I wasn't hallucinating. When I did, it completely stopped. *What in the world is happening?!* I wondered, trying to fit this experience into some grid of my understanding. Though He didn't say so, I had a deep knowing that I could continue testing out my command of the wind. I tried it out two more times—telling the wind to blow and then to stop blowing—and the result was exactly the same.

Then the Lord spoke again and said, "OK, it's not a toy."

I knew exactly what He meant. The lesson was over, and I wasn't to take it too far.

Immediately, I started questioning whether it had really happened to me or if it was some sort of dream or illusion. I find this is pretty normal after experiencing something "unbelievable." A thought starts speaking to me, saying, "That didn't really just happen."

So, to test it, I told the wind, "Don't blow at all until I leave." Then I sat on the bench for another twenty minutes and talked to the Lord without the slightest hint of a breeze. The very second I stood up, turned, and took my first step to leave the park, the wind began to blow again. I was blown away.

I have very little explanation for this experience, other than my belief that the school of the Holy Spirit is the best place to learn. Jesus commanded the elements, and He wants us to know how to do it, too. How amazing that He invites every one of us to be taught personally by Him! This wasn't superhero training, since there are no superheroes in the Kingdom; it was a lesson in obeying Him and stepping into my authority as a son of God.

Going Up

One evening, while I was laying in the bathtub, just relaxing and hanging with God with no real agenda or expectation, He told me to ask Him to take me somewhere.

My first thought was, *Why would You tell me to ask You something?* But I'm finding He does that kind of thing a lot. As I read the Scriptures, I see He did it to people a lot back then, too.

So, I did. I said, "Take me somewhere." I was already very engulfed in the presence of God, but as soon as I said those words, He locked onto my head from the front, on my forehead, and immediately I was in a trance.

I really don't know how to explain this in human language, but I will give it a shot. Everything went dark, and I felt my spirit detach itself from the rest of my being. As soon as that happened, I felt my spirit begin to move, and it accelerated with such force that, while my physical body lay still, my spirit was being thrust forward (or what I perceived to be forward), with such great force that it almost hurt. Kind of like what a roller coaster feels like or what I imagine it feels like to ride in the cockpit of a fighter jet.

All I could see was what I would describe as a sort of wormhole that I was weaving through. Time and space were no longer something to be considered, and I had a deep knowing that we were far outside that realm. While this experience was frightening in the sense that I was definitely not in control, it was also fun because the Holy Spirit was taking me on a ride, and that is just cool.

At some point the speed slowed down for a minute and then took off again until I popped out what I can only describe as "the other side," where I saw four legs walking. Everything else was blurry. As my vision began to clear, the Holy Spirit told me I was on the plains of Africa. Immediately, I recognized the legs belonged to a hyena walking through some grass across the plains of Africa. The weird thing to me (as if this whole story isn't weird) was the fact that I was looking through night vision. Turns out that was because it was after 1 a.m. in Africa.

After such a wild ride, I had no clue what was going on. I watched as a wildebeest casually strolled by. And I asked the Holy Spirit why He had taken me to Africa.

"Because I need people here," He said.

Gulp! I really didn't want to move to Africa. "Do you mean me?" I asked.

"Just pray for them," He said.

Immediately, I was sucked back into my physical time-and-space reality. It was all over in an instant, and I was back in the bathtub.

A few weeks later, this experience began to make a lot more sense. During a Sunday night church service, as worship was ending, the Holy Spirit said to me, "Let's take a walk."

I hesitated for a moment, then stood up, walked out of church, and sat on the front steps. My perch overlooked historic Carrollton Avenue where mature oaks boldly stand their ground and offer shade for the sidewalk and streetcar line that cuts the street in two. I had been asked to take a walk and was waiting for further direction. As I sat and observed, a man across the street, facing my direction and taking pictures, caught my eye. I assumed he was a tourist doing what tourists do—take pictures.

Some time passed without me hearing anything, so I stood up, believing I would hear as I went. I headed down the steps and turned around the right side of the building, headed away from the main street. As I walked along the

56

side of the building, the Holy Spirit asked me, "Why are you going that way?"

"I am just heading in a direction waiting for direction."

"You're going in the wrong direction," He said, asking me to turn around and go the other way.

Once I was back on the correct course, I headed past the church in the other direction, down Carrollton Avenue. Looking at every passing person, I asked the Holy Spirit, "Him? Her? Them?"

Each time, His response was, "No."

Halfway down the block, I saw a man approaching who seemed to be headed toward me, as if he wanted to see me. Soon he was close enough for me to recognize him as a man who went to the church. I had seen him around, but we had never really had the chance to get to know each other.

We greeted each other and made that connection, and I asked him if everything was alright. He told me he had been across the street taking pictures for the church and noticed me sitting on the steps. Instead of leaving for his next destination, he felt led to turn his car around, park it, and walk over to me. He said he assumed he was supposed to check on me because I was alone outside the church during the service, and he wanted to make sure I was OK.

As he told me this, the Holy Spirit whispered to me that this interaction was the reason He had me depart from my seat in the pew.

We chatted a bit, getting to know each other, which was easy and pleasant because he was a sweet and genuine man. Eventually he told me he and his wife had for years felt a call to overseas ministry and had started to pursue it years ago, but never to the extent he believed they one day would. He told me it was actually a strong topic of conversation among them at that time, and they were waiting on leading from the Lord. I encouraged him and prayed for him, assuring him that God would do just that—lead the way.

Then, after we hugged and turned in our respective directions to part ways, the Holy Spirit caused a sudden flashback in my mind to my experience in the bathtub a few weeks prior. Turning around, before he was out of the reach of my voice, I said, "Have you considered Africa?"

Bingo! There it was! Emphatically, he said, "Yes!"

What followed was a whole new spin on the situation at hand. Africa was in fact the place he and his wife had nearly moved to in years prior and were again considering at that current time. Feeling burdened anew for Africa, they had begun discussing how to actualize their call. Should they do a short term trip? Or should they move there to live among the people and start new lives as missionaries? They weren't totally sure, but they knew God had given them a passion and desire for the people of Africa.

Following our conversation, this man went home and shared this divine run-in with his wife. The following week they met with the pastors of the church to discuss this burning in their hearts. Within months, she was on a trip to Africa, spending time in the place she felt called to. They are continuing to trust that God may one day send them there permanently or, if not, send them there often, as He has already begun to do.

That out-of-body experience and the events that followed completely rocked my world. I could hardly believe what had happened. But it was just the beginning. It wasn't long until another encounter of a very different sort changed everything—again.

The Appearing

It was a chilly fall evening. The sun had almost completely gone down, leaving our house dark. A small, yellow lamp warmly and dimly illuminated the windowless room where I sat. One room over, Shannon and our son, Noah, sat in our bedroom happily watching a kids' show on the computer. It was Sunday, and I had to go back to work early the next morning. I felt like mindlessly relaxing by watching the Sunday night football game. Instead, I decided to find out what the Lord was up to, because, all day long, I had felt a tugging deep within my soul that I really didn't understand. I felt uneasiness, but not in an evil sense; this uneasiness came because I sensed Him tugging at me and luring me out of my comfort zone.

I began to pray and thank the Lord for being awesome and for just being Him. As I enjoyed Him, I escaped deeper and deeper into Him until I was immersed in His loving presence. It was the safe, peaceful, and warm embrace of two lovers. I was completely unprepared for what happened next.

As I sat and basked in the glory of my wonderful Daddy, without any warning, Jesus appeared in front of me. He didn't look like He's described in the Book of Revelation (as He appears to some people), Jesus in His glorified state with white hair like snow, eyes of fire, feet like burnished bronze that were refined in a furnace, and a voice like a roar. The Jesus who appeared to me was Jesus hanging on the cross.

The movie *The Passion of the Christ* reminded the Church that Jesus' death on the cross was far more violent and traumatic than the images we commonly see. It showed us what a torturous experience could actually do to a human body. But even the graphic images of that movie did not compare to what I observed that evening. In the vision, I saw Him from the waist up, facing me, but slightly turned to the right. Immediately, I jerked away in shock and tried to look the other way, not wanting to see the horrific image that had so unexpectedly appeared to me. At the same time, I was drawn to Him and could not look away.

His body, which may as well have been a carcass, was draped on the wooden torture device, and His mangled flesh was not even distinguishable as human flesh anymore. He was scourged, beaten, and bruised so badly that His entire body was black and a purplish blue as if He had been covered in gasoline and set on fire for about three minutes, only to have the flame extinguished prior to death. His face didn't even have distinguishable features. It was a swollen and contorted blob, beyond recognition.

He was not hanging in a physical state of peace, like we so often depict. Rather, His body was in shock from the pain inflicted on Him, to the point that He was convulsing. These convulsions were beyond His control, and every time He convulsed, His body seized forward. When that happened, it tore the wounds of the nails holding Him to the cross. It was a constant cycle of agony. As I watched Him struggle, my heart melted with compassion. *Am I really watching Jesus suffer on the cross?*

Finally, after many gut-wrenching, failed attempts at composure, He paused and, with great purpose and authority, took a deep breath and lifted His head. With complete calmness and control, He turned His head toward me. *What is He going to do?* I wondered. His eyes were not the eyes of a man who had given Himself over to be destroyed. Rather, they burned with love, forgiveness, compassion, mercy, and grace. His eyes locked with my eyes. As He stared into my eyes with great intensity, He simply said, "I love you." Then He disappeared.

Until that day, Christ's crucifixion and resurrection had not held the importance they deserved in my life. In fact, it wasn't until several months after this experience that they really did. The very Son of God had appeared to me and allowed me to see part of the agony of His sacrifice of love for me. It was an undeniably important moment in my journey, one that would define everything that followed.

The Longest Bridge across Water

Chapter 5

The Stuff, Part 1: Healing Power

Because as He is, so also are we in this world.
—1 John 4:17

After visions and supernatural encounters began, the next step along my journey into the Spirit was an activation of God's healing power. Thus far, He had focused on my heart and taught me to know and love Him deeply. Now it was time to start spreading that love to the people around me.

First He began to show me that we, as His children, are all His chosen ones, especially called to accomplish His will on planet earth. What an incredible reality! We have been called to walk in the Spirit and, by faith, actualize His will on earth as in Heaven. In other words, we get to walk in power and accomplish crazy wild exploits just as Jesus did when He walked the earth as an example for us.

Amazingly, as we grow in faith and belief, we effortlessly begin to manifest the life flow of Christ. It's that simple. Unless we are impeded by some outward force or teaching, we naturally carry His realm with us into every circumstance. As a result, supernatural events (healing, miracles, prophetic, words of knowledge, etc.) occur. Whole books have been written to explain the theology behind these supernatural gifts, as well as all kinds of manuals to help people mature in them. That's not my purpose here. Instead, I'm simply going to tell you how it happened for me, starting with supernatural healing.

I had read many times the apostle Paul's declaration about his own ministry:

My message and my preaching were not in persuasive words of wisdom, but in demonstration of the Spirit and of power, so that your faith would not rest on the wisdom of men, but on the power of God (1 Corinthians 2:4–5).

I didn't question whether those things had happened in Bible times. However, had someone told me a few years before that I would be walking through the French Quarter with what felt like electricity pulsing through my body, approaching complete strangers, touching them, and watching their bodies be healed as the surge ran down my arm, out of my hand into them, and actualized healing— I'm not sure what I would have said. I *know* I would not have believed it.

Needless to say, I was not pursuing a healing ministry. Instead, it was more like I was dragged willingly into healing by the leading of the Holy Spirit. The way He chose to teach me was first through experience, which He later backed up through Scripture and a solid theological framework undergirding and making plain the why and how of healing. However, before I understood any of that, I began to see people healed when I prayed for them.

With time, I concluded (like many others who regularly demonstrate God's healing power) that it is and always has been God's will for all to be healed. It is hard to operate in faith for healing if I don't believe I am operating within the will and desire of God. Otherwise, I am just begging a mean God who inflicted a sickness upon a person in order to teach a lesson—and hoping my begging will cause Him to change His mind and reverse the curse. That just doesn't make sense. For this reason, it has settled in my heart and soul that God does not inflict sickness and disease upon people, and it is always His desire that they be healed and set free. Whether or not it is my job to play a role in actualizing that in their particular circumstance is for Him to decide and lead. It is my job to be available and obedient to His leading. This understanding, as I mentioned, came with time.

First came the simple belief that Jesus said I would see the Kingdom of God. For me, that promise was enough to step out and believe I could do what He had done. And amazingly, the stuff began to happen, just like He said it would.

That's not to say everything has worked out perfectly. Yes, as I've grown and developed in faith for healing, I have seen and learned some really wild stuff. I have also experienced let-downs and faced the unexplainable times when people are not healed. I used to get discouraged and see those as a failure; now I realize that taking responsibility for the lack of healing is very much like taking credit for the healings. I know the credit isn't mine to claim, and that helps me to keep walking forward in faith, trusting God's goodness even when I don't understand why things happen the way they do.

That's my very simple backdrop to the healing power of God that began to manifest in my life. Now for some really great stories.

Ready Go!

One Sunday night, during a church service, I felt the Holy Spirit tell me someone had a heart condition. Later, I found out this is called a "word of knowledge." I asked the Lord to tell me who it was so I could minister to that person, but I got nothing. Feeling disappointed by the lack of leading, I told a friend after the service about my experience. We were standing in front of the empty church building and were the last ones there.

Just minutes after I mentioned this to my friend, a homeless man and woman walked up to us and asked us for some help and a ride to the man's mother's house. There, they said they could pick up a meal before heading on their way. After chatting with them briefly, we agreed to give them a ride. On the way to the car, I was talking with the man, Gene, and he mentioned he had congenital heart failure. Immediately I recognized what was happening. I told him God had just told me about it, that I was going to pray for him, and God was going to heal him. So when we dropped them off, I prayed for Gene before he got out of the car.

A few weeks later, in my time of prayer, God mentioned Gene to me. "Gene is homeless, God," I said, "and I have no way of getting in touch with him. If You want me to see Gene, lead him to me.

A few days later, he found me. A friend and I were having any early morning meeting at a Starbucks, and my friend (who had arrived first) decided to sit outside. That would not have been my choice because of the extreme New Orleans humidity. Turns out it was God. After going inside for my coffee, I walked back out and noticed a man walking his bike past the coffee shop. It was Gene!

He came over and happily told me that the day after I had prayed for him, he went to the doctor to have tests run on his heart condition. His heart, which had only been functioning at 30 percent prior to the prayer, was now up to 60 percent functioning. I prayed for him again, and then he told me how excited he was he had run into me because his niece Cynthia was unable to walk and in extreme pain due to a very bad back condition. He had been asking God to bring him to someone who could pray for her and heal her.

I told him, "Gene, I'm coming to your house today! God is going to heal her, and I am taking her crutches home with me, and I am going to hang them on my wall!"

Gene and I made arrangements for me to pick him up after I finished work that day. Then we would go to his sister's house, where Cynthia lived.

Later, on my way back from work, God spoke very clearly to me and told me to hold out my hands. He said, "In your right hand I am placing fire, and in your left hand I am placing a hammer" (turns out, that was Jer. 23:29). He then showed me how the events were going to unfold.

When we walked into Gene's sister's house, I saw Cynthia lying pathetically on the couch, a look of misery on her face and a little port-a-potty and a walker next to her. Compassion rose up in my spirit. After getting to know the family who were all gathered in the living room where Cynthia lay, I asked a few basic questions about her condition, which they had very few answers for. She had had surgery in 2003, but they gave no detail about what was done. I told the family we were going to have a sort of worship service. So we prayed and worshiped for a few minutes, and then I told them it was time to pray for healing.

Then ministry time began. We prayed for a while, and as we did, the look on Cynthia's face became increasingly hopeful, yet confused. Eventually she told me her pain was starting to leave, and she was able to sit up for the first time in weeks. I continued to speak to her condition, and moments later she was able to stand with the support of the walker. As she leaned on the walker, I saw a vision of a screw being turned. I told them what I'd seen and asked, "Why didn't you tell me Cynthia has screws in her back?"

Before they could answer, I said, "God is turning the screws and fixing her back right now!"

Right when I said that, her left leg jolted and kicked, and instantly she was healed! She was able to walk without assistance and without problems. We all praised the Lord together and worshiped Him for being so awesome. Months later, I called to see how Cynthia is doing, and her mother apologized, saying Cynthia couldn't talk because she was out jogging! I'm pretty sure that was the best excuse for not coming to the phone I've ever heard!

At the Office

Another time, while I was hard at work at my desk, someone came up behind me, tapping me on my left shoulder.

"Jeremy, I need you to come heal someone," he said.

I swiveled around to find John. Though I was surprised by his request, I was absolutely up for the task. I felt excited that someone in upper management would welcome this kind of thing. John is a wonderful man of faith, and he and I had often discussed the supernatural at length. He was now eager to see if all the talk had any legs.

He closed his office door behind me; I was greeted by Joe, a stocky man of medium height who wore shorts, a baseball hat and a skeptical expression. Introductions were made, and Joe told me he had terrible pain in his left shoulder due to a botched surgery over a year prior. In addition to the pain, it had significantly limited his range of motion and mobility.

He added, "I know I'm not going to be healed, because when I'm injured, I'm injured, and I'm a tough customer."

"That's fine," I told him. "Let's just see what God wants to do."

He reluctantly agreed, and we sat side-by-side in the two guest chairs opposite John, who sat in his office chair on the other side of the desk. I was on Joe's left hand side. I turned to Joe and told him I would start by praying just because I like talking to the Father, and, following that, I would turn to him, place my hand on his shoulder, and talk to his shoulder.

Again, he reluctantly complied after informing me, "I don't let people touch me and pray for me, especially people I don't know, but I'm making an exception because I trust John."

I just smiled and started praying. When I was done, I turned to my right, gently placed my hand on his left shoulder, and spoke to his shoulder. While doing this, I saw an open vision of his nerves within his arm, and I saw pain in the form of light shooting down into his hands.

"Joe," I asked, "does the shoulder injury cause any nerve issues with your hand?"

In a shocked voice, he slowly said, "When you said that, an electric shock just went down my arm into my hand!"

When I asked how his shoulder was feeling, he was too busy staring at John in surprise to answer. But the look on his face and his inability to respond said it all. Eventually he told me the pain was completely gone. He also said that when I was ministering it felt hot and he didn't want me to remove my hand. For a man who wasn't in the habit of letting people lay hands on him, that said a lot.

"My other shoulder's bad, too," Joe said. "You want to take care of that one, too?"

And I gladly did.

When we were done and Joe had left, John and I thoroughly enjoyed watching through John's office window as Joe walked to his car. He kept swinging his arms around as he walked, testing them out, trying to find pain and figure out what had just happened. But all the pain was gone!

Divine Lightening

Not long after that, Shannon and I had the opportunity to pray for our good friend Mary, who was partially blind in one eye. We didn't know all the details of her condition at the time, but later Mary informed me she had had a nodule-like lesion appear in both eyes at the age of six, leaving her left retina blocked. At the age of fourteen, a blood vessel ruptured in the same eye. Her doctors had attempted three procedures to correct the issues. Unfortunately, the surgeries had only worsened the issues and left Mary 90 percent blind in her left eye for the intervening twelve years. It had been very difficult for her, she explained because, robbed of depth perception by her blindness, she constantly bumped into things, cut herself often as she tried to cook, and had to navigate her car everywhere she went doing everything she could to avoid right turns.

When Mary came over to our home for ministry, Shannon and I prayed for a while, with no immediate indication of change. As we continued to pray, I saw a vision of an eye with words bouncing off of it. We decided to keep praying. Moments later, I saw another vision of the same eye, except this time a hand with tweezers was doing surgery on the eye. I spoke out what I saw, and Mary acknowledged that what I had seen was the surgery from years prior, of which we were unaware of at that point. While this greatly increased the atmosphere of faith in the room, there was still no sign of improvement to her sight. I felt the Lord saying that, regardless of what we could perceive in the natural, the work had begun. So, we blessed it and thanked Him in faith in advance.

Over the following weeks, we were all baffled and amazed by the nature of God's creativity and power. At random times during the day and night, I would get a weird sensation in my left eye, and the Holy Spirit would tell me He was working on Mary's eye. I would then text her, and she would tell me she was seeing "lights swirling" and "lightning bolts" in her eye. Each time this happened, the blockage would reduce considerably—from 90 percent to 80 percent to 12 percent to 5 percent. Now there is no blockage at all and only a very slight blurriness that is in the process of being surgically removed by the Great Physician Himself! Incredible.

A Creative Miracle

Each of these stories marks a significant milestone in what I had seen the Lord do through me. In this next story, God once again took me to a new experience of His goodness, this time through a creative miracle. One morning I felt the Lord leading me to go on an adventure. I love when He does that; cool things always happen. At the same time, I found myself fighting nervousness because we always seem to end up somewhere "sketchy."

As I drove, I sang and talked to the Lord. I told Him I was just going to drive and enjoy being with Him until He told me what to do. So that's what I did, and it was a blast. Eventually, He started to lead me in a particular direction.

We live in an area where shootings and robberies often occur, but it seems like the safest place in the world compared to the street where the Lord brought me. Most of the houses were dilapidated and decaying, yet somehow they were still occupied. Poverty and desperation was apparent. As I turned onto the street, I didn't yet know what would happen, but I felt an oppressive force weighing on the top of my car—clearly, my presence was not wanted (the demons weren't happy I was there). This caught me off guard for an instant, I still hadn't gotten the memo about where I was and why I was there, but I quickly got my mind right.

As I continued down the street, I noticed a woman and two kids sitting on a porch. Immediately, the Holy Spirit said "Them! I want you to tell her that I love her, and I want you to give her the $20 bill that is in your wallet."

As I drove around the block to circle back around to the house, I said, "What $20 bill, Lord?"

Then I pulled out my wallet to see that, in fact, I had a $20 bill in there. Apparently I had forgotten about it, but sure enough, the Holy Spirit knew it was there, and He had plans for it.

I walked up to the front porch and, with a smile, said hello and introduced myself. A nervous-looking woman named Patrice greeted me kindly as she anxiously pulled drag after drag from a shaking cigarette teetering between her fingers. I told her God had sent me to her house to tell her He loved her and, while it wasn't much, He wanted to give her a little money to remind her He hasn't forgotten about her.

In shock, Patrice replied, "I almost never smoke, but I have thirteen kids and fifty grandkids, and a lot of them live here in my small house. I didn't know how I was going to put food on my table today, so I was sitting out here asking God for help."

As I listened to her story, I encouraged her with the goodness and love of God, ministering to her soul. She had such a beautiful and warm heart. When she began to tell me of her physical problems, I asked her to stand up, declaring,

"Jesus wants to help you out with the physical issues as much as He did with the money issues."

As Patrice stood, she told me she had horrendous pain in her foot that nearly disabled her from walking. As a nine-year-old, she had accidentally stepped on a sewing needle, which had become lodged in her foot and was still there.

"Why is it still there?" I asked, surprised that a needle would have been left in her foot all these years.

Patrice said, "The doctors wouldn't take it out because it was close to a main vein. They said if they tried to take it, they probably would damage the vein, and I would be paralyzed or have big problems."

I could hardly believe she had lived with a sewing needle in her foot for fifty-one years! Now I was ready to put an end to that nonsense. As she told me her story, my hand had started buzzing with Holy Spirit energy, which is always a sign to me that He is ready for ministry to commence. What followed overwhelmed me with awe at the goodness and creativity of God.

As we prayed, God literally de-materialized the needle and removed it from Patrice's foot so that it disappeared—and she felt it as it happened. I made her search for it, because she knew right where it was and could feel it for all of those years. It was gone now, and she knew it.

As soon as she testified to what had happened, the atmosphere on the porch shifted, and the presence of God fell. He began to tell me things prophetically about Patrice's situation and members of her family individually. I looked at the little girl sitting next to Patrice and told her God was showing me details about how He had gifted her with intelligence that surpasses that of the average person her age. Patrice confirmed it with surprise, explaining that the girl was very advanced in academics. The Lord also spoke some other words to confirm His love and deep desire for Patrice, and I told her about Jesus and about salvation, asking her if she wanted to receive this free gift and become alive in Christ. She eagerly said yes and prayed with me to receive Jesus.

Afterward, I asked her, "How do you feel?"

"New!" she said, smiling.

I told her, "You will never be the same!"

As all this was happening, the power of God continued to spread and flow through Patrice's body and to her hips, which I had not even prayed for. They were healed as well.

Patrice's son then came outside, and she jumped up, so excited to show him what God had done to her foot. His heart was immediately softened, and he received the encouraging words the Lord had for him. He confirmed that the things the Lord had shown me about him were true, and, after we talked for a few minutes about it, he decided he wanted to follow after the heart of God and begin an intimate relationship with the one who was already dwelling inside him. I have much hope for this young man because of his beautiful, sensitive, caring heart and his giftedness—and most of all, because of Christ in him!

As more people came outside, we continued to chat, and God continued to do His thing. I was deeply moved in many ways and thoroughly blessed by all the unexpected goodness that happened on that warm summer morning.

Following Up

This new adventure into the realm of ministry and healing didn't mean my Holy Spirit school was over. Far from it (in fact, I don't think it ever ends), and God used these experiences to not only wow me with His goodness and power but also to teach me and stretch me personally.

The story of my encounter with Ramona illustrates that perfectly.

I had met and prayed for Ramona the Saturday before, and I knew I needed to follow up with her, but I was feeling nervous about it. As I drove the two blocks to my office from my gym, post lunchtime workout, I felt the Holy Spirit pushing me to follow up with her. Then I noticed the dog I had seen Ramona walking when I met her on Saturday. This time, another younger woman was at the other end of the leash.

I slowed the car, rolled down the window, and asked "Do you know Ramona?"

My question caught the woman off guard, and she paused briefly to process. Then her face lit up as she connected the dots. "Yes! I'm her daughter. Are you Jeremy?"

I confirmed that I was indeed the same Jeremy who had prayed for her mother three days prior, and she encouraged me to go to the door of their house, which was across the street from my office, and pay her mother a visit. "She will be very glad to see you," she said.

And she was right. Ramona came to the door and greeted me with the biggest and most sincerely gorgeous smile. She insisted on hugging me, despite my sweat-drenched shirt. All she knew is that God had healed her, and she was filled with joy.

Here's how it all went down. On Saturday morning, I went to my office to read and pray for a bit. The Lord had been talking to me a lot in the previous days, and this particular morning, He continued. As I pulled up to my office building and reached down to grab my Bible and journal, He said, "Leave those there; you're not going to need them."

"Why?" I asked.

All He said was, "You will see."

Considering I was there to read and pray, I found His instructions odd. *Why would God keep me from reading the Bible?* As I was unlocking the glass door to the office, I saw the reflection of a woman across the street walking a little dog with a cone on its head. She was walking with difficulty, supported by a cane. And God spoke again, saying, "Go tell her I love her."

Normally, I love that type of opportunity. It had been several weeks since I had seen anyone healed, and normally I would have been pumped to see a miracle, but I had tunnel vision. My mind was set on spending alone time with the Lord and having Him teach me about walking in the prophetic. Then He threw me this curve ball.

I almost didn't listen. Fortunately, I caught myself and reluctantly obeyed. However, as soon as I turned and walked down the steps toward her, my heart followed. It switched to a new mode of operation, and I saw the woman with the compassion God felt toward her. I approached her and asked if she was having back, hip, and knee problems. She responded in surprise, saying she had issues with all three. Her back was injured, her hip was essentially bone-on-bone, and the meniscus in her left knee was torn.

I said, "I would like to pray for you. Jesus is going to heal you." She gladly agreed.

I placed my left hand on her right shoulder and began to pray a general prayer of blessing and thankfulness to God for paying for her healing. I finished my prayer and knelt down to minister to her knee. All I had a chance to say was "Knee..."

Instantly, her knee popped, causing her leg to jolt and her entire body to shake. The look of surprise and excitement on her face said it all. She had been instantly healed, and she knew it. What an incredible and surprising turn of events for her! As far as she had known, she was just going outside to walk her dog. Then God showed up and zapped her leg, and suddenly she could walk with no pain and no need for her cane. Needless to say, I got an amazing hug before walking back across the street to my car.

Considering the amazing things that had happened on Saturday, I didn't understand why I felt nervous to follow up with her. The truth was, I didn't want to hear that perhaps the pain had returned. When she opened the door and grabbed me, hugged me, and told me she was doing great, my soul leapt with joy. She told me she had gone back to the doctor earlier that day. There the orthopedic specialist who had diagnosed her with a torn meniscus told her that not only did she no longer need surgery but her meniscus was perfectly fine. The pop she had felt in her knee was God mending her knee back to its original position.

She then told me her right hip was still bothering her, and the doctors had told her she needed a hip replacement. We agreed that, since God had already miraculously healed her knee, praying for her hip would be the appropriate thing to do.

"You're not going to believe this," she said as I prayed. "I can feel something shooting down my leg. It's the funniest feeling."

The power of God was pulsating down her leg, starting from the point of the damaged hip. I told her to try walking on it to see if it was still grinding the way it had just before praying.

"No!" she exclaimed, as she squatted repeatedly and walked back and forth down the sidewalk with no pain.

I learned so much through this experience. God really did want to tell her He loves her, and He wanted to restore her broken body. It is so wonderful to be used as the hands and feet of Jesus.

Being a conduit for the love and power of God is an amazing and humbling privilege. Who knows what God will lead us to do if we are willing to listen to Him—even if it means not doing our quiet time?

Chapter 6

The Stuff, Part 2: Prophecy

Pursue love, yet desire earnestly spiritual gifts,
but especially that you may prophesy...
—1 Corinthians 14:1

Not only did God begin to use me to release His healing power to people, but also to speak His words. The Bible calls this prophecy, and I love it.

One Saturday morning while I was at the gym—headphones snug in my ears, pumping out my third set of shrugs, facing the mirror—I was distracted by a man who entered. When there is only one other person besides you in the gym, you tend to notice when a third party joins the mix. I watched via the reflection of the mirror in front of me. The man looked tough and even visually intimidating. Focusing back on my set and the music I was jamming out to, I decided to mind my own business and not stare at people.

That didn't work. Moments later, this man ended up on the bench behind me, and I snuck a glance to find him looking very serious and almost mad. As I began my next set, an open vision popped up in front of my face. I saw the man sitting at a table with books, papers, and notebooks in front of him. His head was down in his hands, and he was rubbing his head in a manner which shouted that he was entirely overwhelmed. This was not an image I would have expected to see of this tough-looking gentleman.

Silently, I asked the Lord if I should do anything about what I had seen and, if so, what. He told me to introduce myself, promising He would lead me from there. That is one frustrating yet fun aspect of situations like these. Often the Holy Spirit only gives me a blip, as He did here. Only when I begin to speak does He put the rest of the words in my mouth.

I really enjoy talking to people, but always have to fight nervousness when I approach people and introduce myself with a purpose of loving them but carrying with me knowledge of something about them that I have no earthly way to know. It is almost an art developed by experience. I've learned just a little about how to do this in a not weird, not awkward way in which the person feels loved, protected, and not exposed.

So, I was pleasantly surprised when, after I introduced myself, he responded with a big bright smile and warm words. I felt led to just go ahead and share with him what I had seen and not beat around the bush. It went better than I could have hoped or imagined; as soon as I shared what the Lord had shown me, this man said he felt so touched that God cared so much about him. Turns out this gentleman was an electrician working for the union; he couldn't retire yet, even though he was just about that age, and all of his friends and co-workers were retiring all around him. He figured if he still had to work a few more years, he may as well work toward getting a desk job so he could get some relief from the oppressively hot New Orleans summers. In order to achieve this, he was studying to become an engineer for the union and hopefully achieve a more desired open position.

This, he explained, was what I saw in the vision—him sitting at the table stressed out and worrying about one of the biggest tests of his life which was two months away. The results of the test would determine his future.

I told him, "God shared this with me because He cares more about your test than even you do, except He isn't worried."

As I talked with him and listened to his story, the love of God deeply touched the man, impacting him more than my words could on their own. Before my eyes, his countenance shifted as he felt the strengthening and encouragement of the Holy Spirit.

This is the beauty of prophetic ministry. We get to be God's love letter to people. We get to share God's encouraging words and remind people of His great love for them.

His Daughter

Another fun prophetic experience also occurred at the same gym. As usual, I was minding my own business when the Lord drew my attention to a man and said, "Daughter." Sometimes all He will give is one word—that's it! Just one stinking word!

I enjoy and am thankful for the opportunity to do things with the Holy Spirit, but I just wasn't feeling it that time. Plus, the whole one word thing left me worried I would end up looking stupid. So I decided to play a stupid game with God. (Don't do this, by the way.) I told the Holy Spirit that if He really wanted me to talk to this guy, He should have him come all the way across the gym to me.

Seconds later, the guy stopped what he was doing, made his way across the gym, and set up shop directly next to me on the adjacent machine. I'm not proud of this, but instead of quickly obeying, I told the Lord that if He gave me the words to say, *then* I would talk to the man. I then moved on to a new spot for my next exercise.

By the time I arrived at the next machine, the gravity of my foolishness had kicked in, and I apologized to the Lord. I asked Him to confirm that He wanted me to talk to this guy by having him come over to me. Again, only a short moment later, there he was, heading my way.

This time, I did what I should have done from the beginning—embrace him in communication and let the river of life flow into him. After introducing myself, I told him I sensed he was burdened by some things about his daughter. Keep in mind, I had never met him before, and I didn't know if he had any kids or, if he did, whether any were daughters. Situations like that could be a tad sketchy, but they don't have to be. This one sure wasn't.

His face went from half disinterested to fully engaged in the blink of an eye.

"How did you know that?!" he asked.

"The God who loves you more than you know wants you to know it is important to Him, and He is working on your behalf to fix things for you," I said.

Then, I got the story. He told me he was finalizing a divorce. He and his ex-wife were in the throes of a nasty custody battle over their two-year-old daughter. He felt he was getting the raw end of the deal so far. In his words, the courts had favored the mother with no cause, and he only got to see his daughter twice a month for a few hours under supervision. Normally, if I would hear this kind of story, I would tend to not buy it, but this time I totally believed him and cared for him.

And he was deeply impacted by the notion that the loving Father of all was interested in this issue that burdened him so deeply. I shared some encouragement and the good news of Jesus with him, and before he left, he gave me a big handshake and told me he was leaving just then for his allotted time with the daughter whom he loved and missed so much.

Monroe Street

Another time as I sat in my prayer chair in my office in the early morning getting direction for my day, the Holy Spirit told me very specifically what street to go to and showed me a picture. I had never heard of the street— Monroe Street. After finishing my coffee, I set off in my car and headed to the neighborhood where this street is found, known as Hollygrove, the childhood neighborhood of the famous musician, Lil Wayne.

As I drove down Monroe Street, I passed a man who was weed whacking in a front yard. Just as I passed him, the Holy Spirit said very loudly and very clearly, "I want you to tell him what is on his mind."

"I can't tell him what's on his mind because I don't know what is on his mind," I said.

I knew, of course, He wasn't going to tell me that until I turned my car around and engaged the man in conversation. As Psalm 81:10 says, *"Open your mouth wide and I will fill it."* So I did just that. After I got his attention, he turned off his weed whacker, and I started talking. Skipping the small talk, I told him right away that the Lord had stopped me while driving and instructed me to talk to him, and then I told him what the Lord had said. (I'm leaving out the details of what I told him for his privacy.) As I spoke, his eyes welled up with tears, and a wonderful, life-filled conversation ensued.

He said, "This has to be from God, because you have no possible way of knowing that other than Him telling you."

We talked about the goodness and grace of God. The Lord told me the man had been born again as a child, which he confirmed, but that he had very little understanding of what it means to be a son of the Most High God and to be the righteousness of Christ. So I talked to him about his identity in Christ and then held his hand and prayed with him. Afterward, he asked for my contact information so we could stay in touch and talk through this further. The part that nearly moved me to tears happened when we were saying goodbye. This tough-looking man in his late 40s looked me in the eyes with the deepest sincerity and said, "I love you. I love you for doing this."

Even as I type this, my heart goes out to that man with such intensity, but I have so much hope for him personally and for his situation because of the unsuspecting encounter he had with God that day.

In all three of these stories, God used me to speak encouraging words to people who really needed to know that God knew and cared about the details of their lives. This is one of the most basic forms of prophecy, a gifting in which all believers are invited to participate. Another way in which God often uses prophecy is related to supernatural healing. Here's the story of how I started seeing and feeling what ails people before they tell me.

Supernatural Knowledge

Early in my journey in the Spirit, while I was at a charismatic meeting, something peculiar happened to me that would soon become my norm. The sermon had ended, ministry time had just begun, and I was listening to the speaker give instructions. Without warning, I began to see inside the body of a teenager standing directly in front of me. His spine lit up and was glowing with an almost bluish tint.

A moment later, the speaker announced that she would be calling out certain conditions and that people with those conditions should come up to the front to receive ministry. Amazingly, the very first thing she called out was back conditions, which I had just seen. To me, this was crazy. I had never had anything like that happen to me, especially not in a corporate setting. Most of my prophetic experiences to that point had been in private or with a small amount of people. Quickly I realized, *This is really fun!*

A few minutes later, I walked down the middle aisle toward the back of the auditorium, on my way to the restroom. About half way back, I felt a sharp pain in my lung. At first, I was caught off guard and surprised by the sudden and unexpected jolt of pain. Then the Holy Spirit reminded me of what He just showed me with back issues. *Oh,* I thought, *this is a word of knowledge. That must mean someone is having lung issues. Let's wait and see.*

When I returned from the restroom, the speaker was nearly done with ministry time. Just as I wondered whether I had missed the fun, she called out the final word of knowledge, which she said was for one particular person with lung cancer.

Out from the pews wheeled a woman, tubes tethering her to an oxygen tank on the cart that supported her. She hobbled forward with hope of being healed. Though at the time I was not very familiar with all of this, I knew without a doubt this woman would be healed. While I never heard it confirmed, I am confident that she was fully healed.

That night initiated a new experience for me. At every corporate gathering or service I attended, I began hearing a list of conditions and names and would write them down. It was words-of-knowledge practice. Often I would see visions of people's body parts lift up or feel their conditions in my own body. Because I wasn't leading the meetings, I usually didn't have a chance to announce what I was seeing or feeling, and sometimes I didn't even know to whom the words applied, but the Holy Spirit was training me to be able to minister in words of knowledge. My chance would come soon enough.

Wal-Mart Words

It wasn't long until God took the words of knowledge outside the church building and used them to direct me to people who needed a healing touch from Him. This happened one morning while I was praying. I had a vision of a woman wearing an odd tank top with vertical stripes that were orange and a couple of other colors. She was walking in the aisle of a store, and I knew the store was Wal-Mart. It was a Thursday morning and I had to work, but there was a Wal-Mart close to my office. I had to find out what God was up too.

As I was driving, I got a strong sense that before work wasn't when I was going to run into her but instead I would find her during lunchtime. I played it safe and stopped by on my way into work but, as I suspected, I had no "luck." Lunchtime couldn't come fast enough. I anxiously waited for the noon hour when I could go back to Wal-Mart and hopefully run into the lady from the vision.

Finally, noon came. After driving to Wal-Mart, I nervously walked around for a little while without finding her. By that point, I had had dozens of divine encounters like this with people, but, as a person who doesn't enjoy walking up to strangers, I was still learning to relinquish fear of man. Feeling disappointed, I gave up and decided to leave, hoping the Holy Spirit would help me understand what had happened. As I turned down the last aisle on my way to the exit door, I spotted the weird horizontally striped tank top. Bingo!

The lady was dragging an oxygen tank with wheels on it, but it was not connected to her nose. I politely introduced myself and chatted with her for a few minutes. Then I asked her what her condition was and why she had the oxygen. She told me an artery in her heart was pinched, and often it would cause extreme shortness of breath, thus the purpose of her wheeled accessory. She was very kind, so I asked her if I could pray for her and told her I believed God was going to heal her. I explained to her how He had shown me she was going to be there. She was very receptive and appreciative, and we prayed right there next to the jewelry counter in the middle of the store. Afterward, she told me that as we prayed, she felt the power of God in her body. Unlike many other conditions or injuries, she was unable to demonstrate immediate evidence that she had been healed. I believe she was.

I was learning the value of trusting God. Whether I was given just blip of information or a vast amount of detail, I had to follow through. I wanted to.

Through experiences like this one, I continued to wet my feet in the prophetic with the Holy Spirit's guidance. Turns out He was preparing me for a new kind of prophetic occurrence—revelation about the future.

Seeing the Hurricane

It happened one morning as I was praying in the Spirit. I went into a vision and saw the East Coast of the United States, from the Mississippi river east. Then the vision took on the appearance of a Weather Channel map, and the northeast was highlighted in red. When Shannon woke up, I described it to her and showed her the picture I had drawn of what I saw. It appeared as though a hurricane was going to hit the northeast. I found it weird because, as far as I knew, hurricanes didn't hit the northeast very often, if ever.

As it turned out, the vision was fulfilled three months later when Hurricane Sandy made landfall on the northeastern coast of the United States.

When I found out about it, I prayed, "Father, teach me what my responsibility is and why you show me these things."

This was the first time I had received a prophecy about something on a national or global scale. At first, it felt really amazing to see and hear things of such magnitude, major world events like natural disasters and wars. But at the same time, it was sobering to consider how people's lives were being affected by these horrible events. To be honest, I am still learning what my responsibility is when the Lord shows me future events. One thing I know for sure is that we are now under the New Covenant. The prophets of the Old Covenant, who were tasked with providing warnings of judgment, are a thing of the past. God is not using storms and other natural disasters as signs of wrath and judgment upon the earth. Instead, He has given me (and all of us) the ability to intercede against any horrible events He shows me and to take authority over the elements and command the winds to be still. I know this is at least one purpose in those times when He shows me events in the future.

As with all prophetic revelation in the New Covenant, God's purpose is always for our good, always for redemption and the expansion of His glorious Kingdom on this earth. That's what the prophetic is all about, whether I'm telling a man at the gym how much God cares about his troubles or foreseeing a national disaster.

Biblical Prophetic Ministry

Sadly, a lot of people have no idea what prophecy is for, and some don't even believe God speaks that way anymore. I'm so glad He does, and I'm so thankful for the freedom His words bring. Not long ago, I got to see firsthand what it looks like when beliefs about prophecy get rocked by actual prophecy, straight from the Father. And well, it was amazing. Here's how it happened.

My friend and ministry partner, Dave flew a pair of pastors, long-term friends of his, halfway around the world in order to spend time together and share what God had been speaking. Dave invited me to come along on a four-day trip from New Orleans to Missouri, including three days canoeing and camping on a twenty-six-mile paddle down a gorgeous river through the Ozarks. Despite not being an outdoorsy person, I agreed.

The eight-hour car ride consisted of nearly non-stop power-packed teaching and riveting discussion. Of course, the gifts of the Spirit came up, and, when the prophetic was mentioned, the atmosphere in the car changed. The Romanian pastors told me they did not believe prophetic ministry is for today. They then told me about an outspoken woman in their town who claims to be a prophetess and makes false claims, doing lots of harm and causing division and damage. Because of that, they had a very bad taste in their mouths about the prophetic.

Fair enough, I thought. So I began to explain that New Covenant prophetic ministry, as Paul so clearly states, is a beautiful thing when used to build up, encourage, and edify the Church. "When it is motivated by love and inspired by the Holy Spirit, the supernatural revelation prophecy can provide is unmatched," I said. "Paul even went so far as to say that we all should prophesy!" I then reminded the pastors that it's not good to throw the baby out with the bathwater. The fact that a wacky lady is running around acting stupid does not negate the value of the prophetic ministry as a whole. "Imagine if, every time a pastor did something dumb, we decided pastoral ministry was no longer relevant and all of the Scripture about it is to be passed over," I said.

The pastors listened politely, and the conversation seemed to be the beginnings of breakthrough in this area. However, I was not content with just talking about it. I asked the Lord for an opportunity to demonstrate prophecy to these pastors.

After we returned from an enjoyable time along the river, Dave brought our Eastern European brothers by my house so we could pray over them before they returned home. As I was praying over the second pastor, the Lord began to speak, so I switched over from praying to prophesying. The words coming out of my mouth were not my own; they were kind and loving words from the heart of the Father directed straight at his heart. Tears began to stream down the face of this man who, prior to the Romanian revolution in 1989, had fought as a soldier and was imprisoned and tortured as a Christian. A moment later, I saw an open vision of him lying on his back in bed at night; his wife was asleep next to him, but he was unable to sleep and was worried. A cartoon-style thought bubble popped up above his head, and I began seeing the thoughts, weighing on his heart and giving cause to his worry.

Again, the Lord began to speak. This time, He spoke about the thoughts I had seen in the bubble. He wanted this man to know that not only was He there with him as he lay restless in his bed, night after night, but He cared about these things more than the man did. As I explained all this, his tears streamed forth again.

Moments later, once it was a bit more appropriate, I told them, "That is biblical prophetic ministry."

What a powerful, beautiful way to experience the love of God together. Truly, I have found nothing more thrilling or fulfilling in this life than allowing God to speak and act through me.

The Longest Bridge across Water

Chapter 7

The Call

Before I formed you in the womb I knew you, and
before you were born I consecrated you; I have
appointed you a prophet to the nations.
—Jeremiah 1:5

As I began to experience all this new and exciting supernatural *stuff* on my journey into the Spirit, God began speaking to me about my call. As New Covenant believers, we all share in the inheritance and calling as children of God. In a general sense, we all participate in life in the Kingdom and have equal access to the Father and every good gift through His Son, Jesus. The Church is in the midst of a revolution of what ministry means and is supposed to look like, and it's a lot different than what we as the church have allowed ministry to become. It is a wonderful and exciting revelation that a businessman can be as much of a missionary as a pastor. We are ALL called, empowered and sent to minister, not simply those who have a Roman collar or an "M.Div." tacked on to their signature. This is the universal call of all believers, to walk in the authority of the Kingdom and be about the King's work.

However, we each also have a specific call which defines how this universal call is walked out in our lives. God had just turned my world upside down when it came to understanding what it means, in a universal sense, to be a

Christian and advance His Kingdom on earth. Now He began speaking to me about my personal calling, disrupting all the notions I had held up to that point. Like Jeremiah, the man I'm named after, I was somewhat abruptly informed by God of my life call.

Our life call is something God placed in our hearts long before we were born. We sense it, but often do not discern it, and, if we do, many times we run from it. I know I did. Then God called my name and told me my destiny. There is nothing sweeter than hearing your name spoken by God. When He reveals to you who you are and what He has created you to be, a sense of security will come over you, and you will never want to be someone else. You will realize you are uniquely made, and you will never look at another person and desire to walk in that person's anointing and call.

Before, I was never particularly happy being myself. Being someone else always had more appeal. But when God revealed my identity to me, I felt completely content just in being me for the very first time. It is amazing to no longer look at other people and wish I had what they had or could be who they are. I get to be me. And that's amazing!

And So It Begins

The experiences I have shared thus far in this book do not relate specifically to the calling on my life. I am convinced that all of us, due to the life of Christ inside us, can encounter Him in various wild and exciting ways. But as my time with the Father developed and I began to know and understand what He was saying, the call began to be loud. He showed me that what I was always created for was *not* the life of marketplace ministry I had desired. This is how it happened.

My usual daily commute, a twenty-six-mile journey across the longest bridge over water in the world, was typical that particular morning. To the eye, everything appeared as it did the day before. However, the atmosphere in the spirit realm was quite the opposite. The drive seemed effortless, almost nonexistent, as I drove mile after mile singing, praying, and prophesying to the city that was rapidly shrinking behind me in the distance.

Overwhelmed by the presence of God, I hardly know how I made it nearly the entire distance of the bridge. Then God spoke to me something completely unexpected. The external audible voice of God (not the still, small voice we often hear) boomed in my car. This wonderfully scary voice spoke words I will never, ever forget: "Jeremy, stop being an accuser of My Church and start being an encourager of My Church."

Hearing the voice of God in such a powerful, external way was both amazing and convincing. But I wasn't quite sure what to do with what I had heard. My mind quickly flashed to the Book of Acts, where Paul was on his way to Damascus when God apprehended him and told him to stop persecuting Him. At that time, Paul was invited into his call to be an apostle by the will of God.

I don't know for sure how Paul felt hearing those words from God, but I do know that, when God spoke so clearly to me, I took it very seriously. I now know this was the beginning of my call. Following that morning, a series of additional "destiny experiences" happened through which God further explained who I am called to be and what I am called to do. They are experiences I hold dear to my heart. The long and short of it was that God wanted me to quit my day job and jump into full-time ministry, with no guaranteed paycheck.

At the time, my job supported our family of three, and I felt very nervous about letting it go. But the longer I put off notifying my employer and making it official, the more visits I received from the Lord, and His tone became increasingly stern—not mean or condemning, but lovingly stern. "It's time," or "It's going to be OK," He would say.

So, I did it. I notified my boss that I would like to give six months notice, which would give them time to find and train a replacement for me and give me time to figure some things out. Three months into the six month period, we found out we were pregnant with our son, Elisha. Little did I know that my destiny was quite unconventional.

My Resume

One of the first things God made clear as I stepped out into the grand adventure of my call was that He had not called me to receive any formal training. He wanted to be my teacher. And it's a good thing, too. Seminary is not my "cup of tea," though I do enjoy sitting in the union at the local seminary when I'm writing. I love God's sense of humor in taking "unqualified" people, like me, and enabling them to do wild things with Him.

It is so fun to be invited by Him to step into a life of adventure and have Him tell me specifically not to attend seminary or ministry school but to simply be taught by Him. I don't say that to dishonor these schools. I really appreciate all the good they have added to the Church. But the fact is, that's not the path God picked for me. And fortunately, Jesus is the one who qualifies us, not a certificate or degree; there's *no* substitute for the anointing of God. I found community with the apostles, who were all called personally by God. Once they were empowered by the Spirit, they knew their calling without a doubt even though most of them had no qualifications or training other than what they'd received from Jesus Himself. Yet they ended up doing incredible things they had no business doing (at least according to logic).

Holy Spirit Fundraiser

When I gave notice to my employer and the paycheck countdown clock started to tick, things began to get very real. This is the pivotal time, for most new ministers, when the planning and fundraising begins. It is almost a rule of thumb in most major ministries or mission organizations that newbies spend a great deal of time within the first year of ministry raising financial support. Then, once a certain income threshold is met, the new ministry spring chicken can begin to do its thing.

However, I was about to discover God was taking me on the unconventional path once again. The same God who had invited me to step away from what I was doing because He had something different in mind for me told me not to raise funds. "What?! Are you crazy?" I asked Him. "You are kicking out every possible financial lifeline." We did not have a single commitment to support us, and I had been forbidden from setting up meetings and sending out letters asking people to support our ministry. He did allow me one exception to this, but it didn't go as well as I would have liked. As it turns out, there was a lesson in it.

But God told me very clearly, "Jeremy, you do what I ask you to do, and I will take care of the money."

As crazy as it seemed, I figured it was the safest place to be; even if it appeared ridiculous from the outside, it was exactly where God wanted me. He had invited me into this ministry thing and told me He would provide; we were just going to have to take Him at His word. Since then, God has only allowed us to approach one individual and ask for support, and that did not go well. I like His method better.

In the six months between me giving notice at my job and my final day at work, the Lord challenged me to see ministry everywhere and at all times. It wasn't just in six months, once it was my "job." No, ministry is clearly everywhere I am. In fact, more ministry happened at my place of work in that six months before I left than had ever happened there before. Had I spent a lot of time worrying about raising funds, I would not have been able to focus on where I was at the time and blessing the people around me.

In lieu of fundraising, Shannon and I say a short, simple prayer for our finances that involves no begging or pleading. It goes like this: "Thank You." We thank Him for the opportunity to serve Him and for His promise to provide. When we have a perceived need, we remind Him of His word and trust that He is fully capable of doing whatever He needs to do to fulfill it, whether by having someone give to us or by providing like He did for Elijah and having ravens deliver food. While He could change this at any time, it is a crazy but extremely fun way to live.

Lesson in a Sandwich

One Saturday afternoon, God further solidified this lesson in my heart. As I often do on hot summer days, I went for a walk around the Bayou to get some sun and hang out with the Holy Spirit. My pace was constant and slow to match my heart rate. I felt relaxed and full of awe at the presence of God. The only thing on my agenda was not having anything on the agenda. It was time to just be.

After two blocks of houses, I reached the Bayou. Freshly cut green grass framed the long, narrow, weaving body of dirty brownish water. Openness is nice. Openness plus water is very nice. Something about bodies of water, even small ones like this Bayou, causes people to want to sit and reflect. Numerous people are always sitting at the water's edge gazing into the distance and pondering who knows what.

Fifteen minutes into my stroll, an older man, probably in his sixties, mumbling unintelligible phrases, wearing a brown suit, a tie, a white plastic cross necklace, and a funky hat approached me. I have gotten used to this sort of thing because, for some reason, I seem to attract these types of situations. I used to get nervous, and my heart would start pumping at an accelerated speed. Not this time. Nothing was going to knock me out of this peace. Plus, why in the world would I not be glad for a chance to love some dude?

I closed the gap between us and was greeted by a request for help and lots of sweat. This dude literally had sweat pouring out from under his hat. I asked him what kind of help he needed, telling him I couldn't do much and pulled out my empty pockets to prove it. I hadn't brought anything with me—no keys, phone, wallet, shirt, nothing! He asked me for some food, asked if I could give him a sandwich or something. I gladly obliged and told him to give me about twenty minutes so I could walk home and meet his request.

Upon arriving back at my house and searching for what was available, I discovered the only option was a peanut butter and jelly sandwich, but it was going to be the best peanut butter and jelly sandwich ever. You can't have a PB&J plain, so I grabbed some pretzels, too. I felt bad that we didn't have any water bottles and I couldn't offer him a drink. However, I reasoned it shouldn't be too hard for him to find some water somewhere else. I figured I would end up sitting with the guy while he ate and building relationship, seeing what the Lord might be up to. After that, perhaps I could help him locate some water.

Casually I strolled back, committed to enjoying the Lord in all the stillness and wonderful peace. Two thirds of the way back to our meeting place, I met the man walking toward me. *Huh?* I thought. *He must have gotten impatient. No worries.*

I greeted him and handed him the two bags. It was obvious he was more interested in evaluating what I had brought than in connecting with me. Holding a bag in each hand, looking down at them, he said, "What do I do after this?"

"What?" I asked, not understanding what he was asking.

He repeated himself, and I got the message. He was pointing out the absence of water. Unbothered, I told him I was sorry I didn't have any water and asked if I could do anything else for him. He quickly shrugged me off and walked away, and as he did, I heard the Holy Spirit chuckle with amusement. Then He said, "Don't let your focus be on your perceived lack. It gets in the way of your gratitude."

Whoa!

He explained that while nothing we do or don't do can qualify or disqualify us from His blessings, misplaced focus will take our eyes off of Him and adversely affect our faith in Him. Before we know it, we will only halfway trust Him to be our provider and just figure we will go elsewhere for the rest and do it on our own. This, He told me, is a form of deception, and we don't even realize we are deceived. We embrace this mindset and don't even know that we have stopped walking in faith.

Whatever She Wants

As I walked away from my job and every safety net was removed, the belief that my Father in heaven truly has unlimited resources and also desires to make them available to me became more and more real. I truly began to find my security in Him, and every day, through every experience of need and provision, He taught me how to believe. God is good to His word. He has met every need. Not once have we lacked. He has always provided for our needs and sent money our way without us needing to solicit it.

Not too long ago, we had yet another experience of supernatural provision. Shannon had been watching a little girl to bring in some extra money for our family, but she really desired to not need to do that so she could focus more completely on being a mom to our son (and the baby on the way). Then one morning God told me He wanted to give Shannon something, and that He would give her whatever she asked Him for. I told Shannon what God had said, and she decided to ask God to provide a different source of income for our family so she could stop watching this other child.

A few months later, the parents of this girl told Shannon they were putting her in school and would not need Shannon to watch her any more. At first, we didn't remember God's promise and Shannon's request. We began to wonder where that extra money (which was a significant portion of our income) would come from. But God strengthened our hearts and reminded us of all the times He had provided for us before. As a couple, we chose to trust Him and not get worried. And then He came through, big time. In the next two weeks, we received unsolicited gifts from people we didn't even know that totaled what Shannon would have earned in four months of watching that girl. We were so blessed and overwhelmed by God's goodness. And by the way, He cares about the seemingly little things, like Shannon's desire to be done watching that girl.

Amazingly, as we finally started to find our security in our Father and His provision, we began to live like we have no limits. My family and I live an extremely humble lifestyle and intentionally keep our expenses very low.

Once I started to catch the revelation of Kingdom finances, what vastly increased was not our personal spending, although that would have been fine, but it was our giving that skyrocketed. We had less security and a bank account with no guarantee of being replenished (other than some wonderful regular donors), but we gave as though we had money. That was new for the formerly scared, religious, and tiny-faithed me.

Of course, it was Jesus, and He is as backwards as He is fun.

Chapter 8

Lessons from Father

*See how great a love the Father has bestowed on
us, that we would be called children of God;
and such we are.* —1 John 3:1

Early on in my journey into the Spirit, as I was rocked
to the core by the love of the Father and the kindness of His
will toward me, I began to see people in Scripture like
Moses, David, and Enoch who had a different view of God
than anyone else. Moses and David had seen His power and
His mighty works, but they knew there was more. They
wanted to see His ways, not just His power, not just His
stuff. As I read their stories, this same desire stirred in me. I
had to know everything about Him, and I was going
straight to the source to find out. My destination was set,
my sights fixed on His heart. I began to pursue Him with
all I had.

How wild it is that now, under the New Covenant, we
have unveiled access to the heart of the Father. The great
men of God of old would have killed, literally, for what we
now freely possess. As I began to take advantage of that
open access I'd been given as a son of God, I started to
learn all kinds of amazing and mind-blowing things about
my Father and His desires for us.

One of the first things I learned is that God loves to give us experiences, and He will do so even in the midst of our lack of understanding and even if we have bad theology. No human on earth has perfect theology, and God understands that. He meets us where we are and pulls us into a greater reality. He is in the business of rocking our worlds and blowing our minds, and He has lots of fun doing it. In fact, He is more eager to give us fun times than we are to receive them.

On the flip-side, the human tendency, after having a profoundly powerful encounter, is to try to duplicate the same atmosphere in order to facilitate the same experience. I learned that the hard way when, without realizing it, I began to evaluate my time with the Lord based on whether or not I saw any cool visions or heard Him tell me anything big. I would sit in the same place, morning after morning, and do things in the same order, hoping He would perform. Now it seems so obvious how silly I was, but at the time, it really didn't feel silly to me. It felt as though I was being holy and seeking God.

He, on the other hand, was about to throw a wrench in my super spiritual morning routine. One morning, He asked me, "Why are you sitting in that seat?"

"This is where I like to sit," I said. It was my usual morning prayer time seat, but He wasn't having it that morning.

"Go take a bath," He said. "I want to talk to you there."

The human mind always wants to predict, understand, and control things—including God. That's just how we are, whether we realize it or not. By telling me to take a bath, God was training me to trust Him and not limit Him by the efforts I was unknowingly making to control Him. This is an ongoing process in our lives. The only limits we have in Him are the ones we self-impose. He wants so badly to teach us how to get free of the poverty of our own expectations so we can, by faith, see the impossible.

All My Why's

As I was soon to discover, a lot of my poverty of expectation was wrapped up in one word—the question "Why?"

Our three-year-old son, Noah, is at a very fun age; learning, growth, and development are exploding within him, and change happens almost daily. As a result, his very favorite question is "Why?" A typical conversation between us might go something like this:

"I love you, Noah!"

"Why?"

"Because you're special."

"Why?"

"Because God made you that way."

"Why?"

And so it continues. Noah, my son, illustrates our tendency to ask "Why?" in those times when we truly want to understand a complex, foreign concept. At other times, Noah asks me "Why?" to test me and try to frustrate me. The testing type of "Why?" is what I want to focus on.

At three, a child is trying to figure out the entire world, which is new and exciting. Noah genuinely needs to ask those questions, and I need to genuinely and lovingly lead him into understanding. There will, however, come a point in time, as he progresses, when he transitions out of asking me "Why?" all the time. He will grow in maturity and understanding, and when I ask him to do something, the reply will be "OK," not "Why?"

Early on in my walk with God, when so much was new and uncharted terrain, I did a lot of asking "Why?"

"Why wasn't that person healed?"

"Why did You ask me to do that, Lord?"

"Why, why, why?"

Somewhere along the way, He showed me that some of my questioning was legitimate, but much of it was placing Him on trial and trying to force Him to explain Himself to me. The crazy thing is that often I asked the question thinking I wanted the answer, but, actually, I was asking the wrong question. He knew it. I didn't because I was too caught up in my frustration which kept me from being able to see clearly.

The Father longs to teach us His ways and His heart, but He wants us to trust Him and approach Him with faith. For me, the question "Why?" would evaporate as soon as I came into His presence, and, instead of challenging Him with my lack of understanding, all I could do was bask in His glory. After repeating this pattern for several months, I realized I had transitioned. I had stopped asking "Why?" because all the answers are answered in His presence. It really is that simple. He is the answer to everything. I used to think that was a cliché and not very helpful phrase, a fake and meaningless cop-out. But it couldn't be more true. He really is the source of everything, the answer for all our why's.

Part of that learning process involved learning not to idolize His experiences or His voice, not to use Him for His stuff. The Holy Spirit began to show me that at times I would go to Him just so cool things would happen. This may seem like semantics, but this realization cut me to the core. I was so sorry I had treated my Father, my best friend, as a means to an end. Once I got that in check, I was able to enjoy Him in an even deeper way.

It all came together one day when I was seeking Him for some wisdom and an answer on what was, at the time, a very big decision. Of course, going to Him was the correct Christian thing to do, right? Wrong! Not that time. What I learned as I went on a walk with Him that day was that He is more interested in us finding rest in Him—because He is the answer—than in giving us the answer we want or think we need. As I stepped out of my house and set off down the street, I told Him I didn't want to go to Him to discuss "stuff" and I didn't want to go to Him as my answer genie. I just wanted to go for a walk with Him and enjoy the fellowship of my best friend.

We ended up having a great time, and, in the following days, I got my answer, but I didn't care. I had Him, and He had me, and nothing else mattered. We had each other, and He was continually teaching me how to walk in the fullness of my identity and destiny. What more could I ask for? With that revelation, I was finally able to begin learning in earnest, with a pure heart. Here are some of the things He taught me.

Through His Eyes

One morning, as I rested in the Lord, He asked me what I wanted Him to show me. I told Him, "I want to see things from Your perspective and see what You see."

He then took a pair of goggles and placed them on my head and prepared me to see from His perspective.

In the instant before I began to see, I imagined what He was about to show me. Of the possibilities, I thought, maybe He would show me how He sees the city or the nation or the world. Perhaps He would show me something gigantic in magnitude, possibly some future event. Not so.

What appeared before me was a single beautiful flower. It doesn't sound very profound, but in fact it was. For the first time ever, I looked at a flower, an object I had seen many times, with the eyes and heart of God. It was weird, because as I gazed at this flower, I was filled with a warm love and concern for the flower. I honed in on every detail with intense focus. I was looking at it as its creator.

I began to understand that in this world of billions of people, trillions of animals, and countless other living organisms, God is currently gazing upon all of them with an intense and fierce love. He feels a concern, but not as we would think of it. Not in the sense of worry. He feels concern in that it matters very much to Him that the flower blooms and blossoms to its intended potential. He allowed me to feel what He felt as the creator of the flower while looking at the flower. It was more than the appreciation a person feels who enjoys the finished product but had nothing to do with its formation.

He then asked me, "Jeremy, if this is how I feel about a flower, how much more do you think I feel toward people?"

As He said that, I saw a vision of a man running from the scene of a shooting he had just committed, and the Lord said, "Even for those who are shooting people and committing crimes, my heart is to see them become who I have created them to be. I don't look at them the way you do, Jeremy."

What a reality check! It is so easy to get caught up in day-to-day activities and act out of routine or obligation or not at all. But He wanted to remind me that, just as Jesus so wonderfully exemplified, He only operates out of love, compassion and mercy. I need to have His perspective and operate with Him. He showed me that His reality and the lens through which He sees people are very different than mine. Even those who are the hardest to love and seem to be the farthest down the path of depravity and hopelessness, He looks at without worry but with a fiercely warm love and concern.

That day, I chose God's perspective and left mine once and for all.

A Father's Perspective

Then God began to show me not only how He feels about people but how He feels about the way we often treat Him. Naturally, one of the ways I learned this was through my earthly experience as a father of two wonderful boys, Noah and Elisha.

Every time I come home, my 3-year-old son, Noah, greets me at the door, telling me something exciting he did while I was away and then giving me a big hug and kiss. I love that greeting. However, one day it did not go like that at all. That day he had no hug and kiss for me, and when I tried to initiate, he informed me he did not want to give me a hug and kiss, and then he tried with all his might to escape my embrace. When I let him go, he ran away.

Honestly, that hurt my feelings. And the offenses continued. Not only did Noah act coldhearted and refuse to receive or give any affection, but he also acted defiant and exhibited an attitude throughout the evening. All I wanted was for my son to receive the love and affection I was so ready to give to him.

The next morning, he woke up at 5:15, and I hung out with him for a little while as Shannon and Elisha slept. After he ate his breakfast and watched a little show, he asked to play with Play-Dough. Until that point, he had only engaged me when he wanted something. I got his play dough out, and he sat at the table and played with it while I made my eggs. Wanting to relate with my son, I said something to him but got very little response.

As I sat and watched him play, I heard the Holy Spirit begin to talk to me. He asked me how it felt to be rejected by my son at the door the evening before and having to deal with his attitude all night, when all I wanted to do was have fun with and enjoy him. He asked me how it felt to only be engaged when my son wanted something from me. He asked me how it felt to watch my son play and, when I tried to talk to him, have him not even acknowledge me.

"It sucks, Lord!" I said.

"This is a picture of how many of My kids treat Me," He said.

Ouch! He didn't say this in condemnation but as an incredibly wonderful invitation. God is looking at us with love that is so profoundly intense that we cannot even begin to understand it. And He wants us to freely receive this love and relate with His heart with faith and boldness, as sons and daughters who are fully righteous, accepted and approved! Everything else flows out of this place. What I learned that day is that if I'm "doing" apart from relationship, I need to chill out and get hooked up to the heart of my Father. Then He will have me press *play,* and I can enjoy the infinite possibilities with the infinite promises and infinite blessings. No whining necessary.

Plan for the City

Along these same lines, one morning I had an encounter with the Lord that personally challenged me, and it has spoken deeply to several others with whom I have shared it. Here's what happened. As I was before the Father, He pulled out what looked like a big rolled-up treasure map. He unrolled it and laid it out, calling it His "plan for New Orleans." He began to adamantly speak to me about it, saying He is looking for men and women who are interested in what He is doing; what He wants to do; and how, when, and where He wants to do it. He was looking for people who are more interested in His plan than their own. He said many people are planning and creating, pursuing their own agenda and calling it His.

But the ones who seek His heart first in the secret place, those are the ones to whom He will give access to His plan, and He will show them what part they play. Then they can co-create and be thinkers and dreamers with Him as they are led by the Holy Spirit. He said many of His leaders in the city had it backwards. He wants to see His sons and daughters accomplish great things in His name. Often people get desires that are godly early on, yet they leave intimacy with God to pursue the vision. He said, "I am not impressed with that, even if the natural man is impressed."

He continued to tell me that He wants us to see and perform great exploits, but they must be done from a place of peace and rest in Him. He wants us to offer the city the abundance of blessing we have received. But it's hard to offer the city light, hope, and life if we are tired and empty spiritually. The reality is, He is giving us an invitation into His heart, and He wants to bless us beyond our ability to ask. He says, "Come to My table and be with Me and eat until you are full. Then we can talk shop."

God kept repeating this theme, over and over, in various ways. Apparently, it was pretty important to Him.

Enjoying Daddy

My next reminder of God's priority on relationship came through a freshly fed and happy baby boy who was handed to me as Shannon ducked away for a little post early morning feeding nap. It was 5:30 a.m., and, as far as this little dude was concerned, it was play time. He hadn't gotten the memo that it was daddy's time to read the Bible, journal, and talk to Jesus.

I poured my coffee and placed Elisha in his bassinet, where he could lounge next to me and I could make sure he was content. Then I opened my journal and began to write my feelings toward the Lord:

Lord, before I get ahead of myself and dive into all of the mumbo jumbo "about You," I want to relate with You and tell You that You are special to me. You truly do never fail. You are always dependable and always guiding me into truth. Even if I am running around frantically with an un-renewed mind, You are right there...

It took several attempts for me to even complete that little blurb, not because I had writers block but because the little smiler in the bassinet was pulling out every cute trick in the baby book, and I couldn't stay focused. He was trying to engage me in all the best ways a two-month-old knows—smiling, flailing his arms around, punching himself in the face, spitting up, and so forth. As I looked down at Elisha again, the love of the Father swept over me with a consuming warmth, and He began to speak to me.

As I sat there on the sofa, leaning over and looking at Elisha, smiling and talking baby-talk, the Father was leaning over my shoulder, looking over both of us. And He gently reminded me of the picture He had shown me the day before.

While I prayed, He had shown me a large room with a bookshelf in it. This seemed normal enough to me, until we started to zoom out. As we did, I was able to see the room contained thousands upon thousands of shelves, which must have held millions of books. I realized I couldn't see the walls because the room was too massive.

"Do you see this?" He asked.

How could I not? I thought to myself and said, "Yes."

He said "You could read all of these books about Me, which couldn't even contain the fullness of who I am, and you still wouldn't know Me."

He then took me to another room, and instead of zooming out, He took me from right to left. We panned across this giant room, and I watched as we passed a sea of old empty school desks. The room had the feeling of being absolutely abandoned by everyone except Him. I sensed the desks shouldn't be empty.

"This is my classroom," He said.

I got the point. I had been doing a ton of reading in Scripture as well as in other books and had been studying almost as if on a mission, because I was doing a lot of learning (and unlearning). Yet prior to this vision, I had sensed God telling me to chill out and take a break from all the learning so I wouldn't lose sight of Him. He wanted me to return to doing what I do best, being His friend and relating with Him. The vision was a reminder that, above all else, the Trinity is a relational God. What God is most concerned with is whether or not I am at rest in unity with Him.

That morning, as the three of us—baby, father and Father—engaged each other in the living room, I realized the beauty of what we were experiencing. I was looking down at my beautiful son who was enthralled with his daddy. His belly was full, his diaper had been changed, and he had no needs other than to enjoy his daddy. Though I am a grown man, this is a picture of my relationship with the Father.

In the midst of financial hardship, people issues, uncertainty, family drama, or whatever, I must not focus on what appears to be the problem because the reality of me and my Father sitting and playing happily, even in the midst of absolute chaos is my greatest and only reality.

This is not an avoidance tactic or a mind-over-matter trick; it is faith and rest in the finished work of Jesus. It is an understanding of what it means to be adopted as a son— that all that belongs to Jesus now belongs to me! My favorite part of the blessing of adoption is my ability to approach and relate with the Father with boldness and confidence and not an ounce of fear.

He told me, "The most spiritual thing you can do at this moment is not read the Bible but relate with and enjoy Me and your son." It still blows me away that He is in no way impressed with the spiritual gymnastics we sometimes do, thinking we are doing things for God or learning about God. Instead, He is just waiting for us to be still and hang out with Him.

Chapter 9

Walking by Faith

Now faith is the assurance of things hoped for, the conviction of things not seen. —Hebrews 11:1

I am not one who naturally enjoys drawing attention to myself. Quite the opposite. I usually make great effort to avoid standing out of the crowd. However, it is unavoidable when, on the top floor of one of the tallest buildings in New Orleans, one works out in the penthouse gym in front of large windows overlooking the city. That was exactly what I was doing one August morning. Shannon and I were attending a marriage seminar held in that hotel, and I had gotten up early to train.

The Lord came to me in this unexpected moment and told me to take off my shoes. *What an odd request,* I thought. But God had been doing some unusual (though awesome) things at the seminar, so I should not have been surprised by His odd request. The night before, while the other couples went to dinner, Shannon and I had eaten a quick dinner before heading into the conference room, where the meetings were held, to pray. During that time, I saw a vision of the empty tables that sprawled out before us. Certain seats began to light up. I knew it must mean something, so I grabbed a napkin and drew the layout and put an "X" on the spots that were lit up. A few hours later, during ministry time, couples who were having a hard time and needed prayer were encouraged to stand up, and people circled around them to pray. As it turned out, the seats I had seen light up in the vision were exactly where the struggling couples were sitting.

God had been talking to me a lot over the course of the prior day, so, when He came to me and told me to take my shoes off, I just went ahead and did so and then continued the final portion of my workout.

Soon I found out the shoelessness would continue longer than I'd first thought. I finished my workout, headed down the elevator and through the hotel to my room, getting ready for the morning meetings. Still hearing God telling me to leave my shoes off, I shrugged off the thought of looking silly, and I just carried my shoes with me in case He told me I could put them back on. I imagined what would happen if someone asked why I was carrying shoes rather than wearing them. The only answer I could think to give was, "God told me to." *How weird would that be?* I thought.

Halfway through the morning session, when I walked out to find the restroom, I asked the Holy Spirit, "OK, why are You having me do this?"

Quickly and nonchalantly, He said, "I am teaching you to walk in faith."

Hmm, I thought. *This is really cool and everything, but isn't there another less weird way to do this?* At least I was finally getting over the weirdness of it and having fun. In a way, it was pretty amazing to have the Lord personally taking interest in showing me a different perspective on life.

The rest of the day included a series of lessons. He delivered one as I exited the comfort of the swanky hotel carpet and marble floor and stepped onto the steaming New

Orleans in August hotel parking lot blacktop. Later, I received another lesson during a walk out of my house, two blocks down the hot sidewalk to the cool grass around the Bayou and then back onto the sidewalk. I found shade anywhere possible to keep my tender little soles from frying.

What did I learn? This walk, my personal life journey, will be a good one. I will face hard times and enjoy good ones, and I will make it through both. God will be with me the entire way. Further, what will keep me going is not relying on my own means but relying on the voice of my Father. When He says, "Take off your shoes," He gives you the grace to walk barefooted where you need to go.

Faith Elixir

This faith, which is the crux of our ability to trust Him on our journey, soon became a main theme in my times with the Lord. He wanted to renew my mind and challenge what I'd always thought about faith. As I listened, He gave me a new perspective on what faith really is and how one operates in it.

One morning, as I was fellowshipping with the Holy Spirit, He said, "Faith is a substance" over and over. Then, He said, as clear as day, "Faith is My elixir."

"What are you talking about, Lord?" I asked.

He responded by telling me to open my Bible to Hebrews 11:1, where it says, *"Now faith is the assurance of things hoped for...."*

Then He told me to look up the meaning of *assurance.* What I found was that it actually means "substance." He then led me to look up the word *elixir.* Here's how *Merriam-Webster* defines it:

1. a *substance* held capable of prolonging life indefinitely

2. the essential principle

After checking a few other translations of the Bible, I found that the New King James translation actually uses the word *substance* rather than *assurance* in Hebrews 11:1.

In other words, faith is what gives us the ability to see the actual substance of what is believed for. Followers of Christ do not walk by feelings, emotions or natural circumstances. Rather, they walk by faith in what God has spoken, even if all the feelings, emotions, and circumstances say otherwise. As Paul said, *"We walk by faith not by sight"* (2 Corinthians 5:7). In other words, we do not live according to what our physical eyes see but according to what faith allows us to see and based on what God has spoken.

Then, moving on in Hebrews 11, I read verse 3: *"By faith we understand that the worlds were prepared by the word of God, so that what is seen was not made out of things which are visible."* God said, "See, faith, My elixir, is what I used to speak form to the worlds."

What?! My brain was having a hard time keeping up.

All the teachings I'd ever heard referred to people using faith to understand. But God told me that, while we do understand via His faith, in Hebrews 11 that's not what He was saying. Rather, He was saying that we understand that He spoke and gave substance to the invisible by faith, making it visible. He spoke, and it was so!

From there, He led me to Romans 4:17:

(as it is written, "A father of many nations have I made you") in the presence of Him whom he believed, even God, who gives life to the dead and calls into being that which does not exist.

Even God, the very one who gives life to the dead and calls into being that which does not exist, speaks and acts by faith. According to God's faith in His word (as revealed through the Son), the world was created from nothing. He spoke it, and it was so, which implies faith in His own power to be able to do so. Therefore, this is what I understand it to mean: By faith God made the world, and by faith we understand that God made the world. As the following passages state, it is *His* faith we are gifted with, which then enables us to operate accordingly.

> *Even the righteousness of God which is by faith of Jesus Christ unto all and upon all them that believe: for there is no difference* (Romans 3:22 KJV).

> *Knowing that a man is not justified by the works of the law, but by the faith of Jesus Christ, even we have believed in Jesus Christ, that we might be justified by the faith of Christ, and not by the works of the law: for by the works of the law shall no flesh be justified* (Galatians 2:16 KJV).

> *I am crucified with Christ: nevertheless I live; yet not I, but Christ liveth in me: and the life which I now live in the flesh I live by the faith of the Son of God, who loved me, and gave himself for me* (Galatians 2:20 KJV).

> *But the scripture hath concluded all under sin, that the promise by faith of Jesus Christ might be given to them that believe* (Galatians 3:22 KJV).

> *In whom we have boldness and access with confidence by the faith of him* (Ephesians 3:12 KJV).

> *And be found in him, not having mine own righteousness, which is of the law, but that which*

is through the faith of Christ, the righteousness which is of God by faith (Philippians 3:9 KJV).

Buried with him in baptism, wherein also ye are risen with him through the faith of the operation of God, who hath raised him from the dead (Colossians 2:12 KJV).

God's faith is faith in Himself, as He is the Author and Creator, the Alpha the Omega, the Beginning and the End. He is the one and only true God who rules and reigns forever and ever.

However, faith is an attribute of God that He gives to us as a free gift, just as He gives us courage, grace, joy, hope, and love. All of these gifts are aspects of His person. Our faith is just a returning of *His* own faith. Just as love originates in God and we are merely recipients and mirrors of His love, so we are recipients and mirrors of His faith.

At first, this seemed absolutely mind-boggling to me. And with good reason. Faith is a mystery. *"They must hold the mystery of the faith with a clear conscience"* (1 Timothy 3:9). The good news is that God makes mysteries available, but they can only be received by revelation knowledge. People who walk by faith do not operate based on what the natural eyes see. Instead, they are giants of faith who live by the revelation of truth they have received from the Holy Spirit. This kind of faith walk is offensive to many, and those who do not understand often view people of great faith as being crazy. That's because faith is not in any way rooted in intellectualism; it is spiritual! And it often does not make any sense at all. It cannot be learned or figured out. It must be received, freely, by revelation from the Holy Spirit.

As the Holy Spirit enabled me to understand what faith really is, I felt overwhelmed by His goodness toward me. And the more I learned about faith, the more accelerated my journey of faith became. The discovery of His mysterious faith inspired in me an even greater hunger to seek God.

Faith and Works

One day, as I was talking with God, He told me, "I give you faith for action. If you do not use that faith, it's dead, and you need to get new faith." He was referring to James 2:17, *"Even so faith, if it has no works, is dead, being by itself."* This subject has caused quite the confusion in Christian circles, but the reality is simple. God provides us with faith so we can take action to accomplish what would otherwise be impossible.

This is further explained in Hebrews 4:2, where it connects faith to ability to hear the word of God:

> *For indeed we have had good news preached to us, just as they also; but the word they heard did not profit them, because it was not united by faith in those who heard.*

The fact that we need faith to even comprehend the gospel shows how much we need it for everything we do. Just like any other gift from God, faith is given to us with an intended use. We cannot have either living and effective faith or works without the other.

Under the Chair

Another lesson on faith began as I heard the Lord say to me, "Look at Romans 4:20–21." I enjoy the Book of Romans and am familiar with much of it offhand, but I did not know Romans 4:20–21, so of course I had to check it out:

> *Yet, with respect to the promise of God, he did not waver in unbelief but grew strong in faith, giving*

121

glory to God, and being fully assured that what
God had promised, He was able also to perform
(Romans 4:20–21).

"Cool!" I said. "Sounds great to me. But why are You telling me about this?"

"Look under your chair," He said, "because there are bills under there for you."

I knew He was referring to money for me, not obligations that I owe. I hesitated and entertained doubt for a quick second. I thought, *If I look under the chair and there is no money, I will be confused and let down, because either I heard wrong or who knows what?* After a brief inner wrestling, I got out of my chair. I tried to muster up my faith, and then I remembered what I actually need is His faith. So I asked for His faith to believe. Halfway filled with faith (and still half full of doubt and nervousness), I lifted the arm of the chair and revealed the bare, bill-less floor staring back at me. Nothing!

Disappointment rushed in. It started to whisper poison to my mind and heart. Feeding these feelings of accusation, I asked the Holy Spirit for an explanation. "What's the deal?" I asked. "Why is nothing there?"

Immediately (thankfully!) God's grace swept in, giving me an understanding deeper than my human reasoning. Suddenly, I got it! It wasn't about the bills. It was about me growing in faith and trust, about me being assured in belief in what He has promised. After backing up, I took another shot at my question, asking instead what He often refers to as "the right question."

"Lord," I asked, "why didn't I see the bills?"

The right question changed everything! It was not about Him being on the stand and facing an accusation to determine whether or not He is good. That has been settled. He is good. It was about seeing from His perspective, seeing through the lens of faith that actualizes His reality. But first I needed to believe He meant what He said. If I didn't experience the anticipated outcome, the lack wasn't on His end.

Faith Actualizes

He began to show me that faith doesn't create or determine things; rather, it is the substance that allows us to see and then actualize or realize what already exists. It doesn't make it so. Healing and salvation already happened; when we believe, they are simply actualized. Faith does not save us; Jesus already did that. Faith simply allows what has already been accomplished in the invisible realm to become manifest in the natural.

When we walk in faith, in the Spirit, we are operating from Heaven toward earth. We then see the world as God sees it, and we cooperate with Jesus to bring into the visible realm everything that already exists in God's unseen realm. We are God's chosen sons and daughters, and our job is to bring into being on earth what already exists in Heaven. We impose His realm upon the earth realm. When we have this mentality and realization, it is simply impossible for us to not walk in the supernatural.

The idea that something can be "so heavenly minded, that it is no earthly good" is a bunch of silliness. The truth is, it is only when we become heavenly minded will that we can accomplish any earthly good. This was the new perspective the Father gave me in preparation for another big shift. A new lens, really. He threw out my old and faulty ideas about faith and gave me His perspective. He made it so clear I couldn't do anything to earn faith and that my Father loves to give faith to me (and you too) and watch me operate in it. It's exactly like the Bible says; we cannot please God without faith (see Heb. 11:6). Now it was time for something new on this bridge into the heart of the Father. I like to call it my second awakening.

Chapter 10

The New Lens

*God willed to make known what is the riches of
the glory of this mystery...which is Christ in you,
the hope of Glory.* —Colossians 1:27

My already astounding and mind-bending journey suddenly got even better. Revelation from the Holy Spirit started to allow me to make sense of many things the Lord had spoken to me at earlier parts of my journey. I hadn't known in those earlier times what He meant. In the beginning, I needed nothing more than the utter excitement and surprise that the God of the universe wanted to relate with me and use me in wonderful and exciting ways. Those earlier days were our honeymoon, if you will.

Now the honeymoon was over, and it was time to go deeper, time to really get to know one another. I knew revelation was on its way. I had been spending a significant amount of time in thought and prayer regarding how to grow in the measure of power I was seeing manifest through me. The fact is, I was not seeing greater things than Jesus did, which was what I had expected to see. After all, that's what He said would happen, and so that's what He led me to expect. I wanted greater understanding, and I wanted Him to remove my unbelief. I was determined to find out what it would take to see what I believed should be happening.

I had already established a solid foundation of relating with God, knowing Him and being led by Him. Now He was leading me into something new, a new level of understanding that would soon lead to a new explosion in my life.

This is how it started.

Five Kings

As I lay there, barely able to move and hoping this moment would never end, the Lord began to show me images I would soon learn were a chronological depiction of the next several months of my life. I was a lion in the vision, and I was moving across particular landscapes and doing particular things that were representative of events to come. In the last event of the vision, I (the lion) was underwater swimming, and the scene panned from a head-on shot to a side shot while I was still swimming.

There was a pause, and the Holy Spirit said, in a very matter of fact way, "Pay close attention." The numbers one, two, three, four, and five appeared, one by one. When the number one appeared, it remained for about half a second; then it faded out and number two faded in. And so forth. This pattern repeated several times. And between each repetition, He asked me, "Did you see that? Did you get it? Make sure you got it." Once this progression ended, the lion came back into focus, and the view panned from the side view to a rear view as I (the lion) swam off into the unknown. Then, it was over.

I was able to comprehend some of the beginning parts of the vision because I recognized them as something that had recently happened; this served as a reference point for the following unknown events. However, I did not understand the meaning of what I had seen for several months. Of course, it was obvious the numbers one through five were quite a big deal, because the Holy Spirit had showed them to me over and over again and stressed that I pay attention to them. I just had no idea what they meant.

Two weeks later, as I was spending time with the Lord one morning, I saw a vision of a Bible open and heard "Joshua 10." I eagerly snagged my Bible and flipped quickly to my destination, wondering what I would find. The heading of the chapter read "Five Kings Attack Gibeon." Because I was not familiar with this passage, the story took on a special life to me; I knew it held a meaning I was supposed to grasp. Here's my summary of it:

Adoni-zedek, King of Jerusalem, led by fear, rallied Hoham king of Hebron, Piram king of Jarmuth, Japhia king of Lachish, and Debir king of Eglon to attack Gibeon after he heard Joshua had made peace with Gibeon after his overwhelming victory at Ai.

The people of Gibeon held Joshua to his word, which they tricked him into agreeing to, and he backed them up in the battle and utterly destroyed the five kings' armies.

The five kings hid in a cave, and Joshua had them sealed in so they could not escape while the rest of their armies were finished off. Then Joshua brought the five kings out and publicly killed them, hanging their bodies from trees until evening. Then he returned them to the cave after stomping on their necks, making a big speech, and telling the people not to fear but to be courageous.

It is a cool story, but I didn't understand what it meant or how it related.

A few weeks later, as I was talking with a dear friend and mentor, I mentioned these events and asked his take on it. Without hesitation, he said, "The names of the kings have meaning. You need to know what they were and what they mean." He said the opposite of the meanings was important too, that they would show me what that name would mean apart from God. Here's what I found:

Adoni-zedek, king of Jerusalem

- Meaning: My lord is righteousness
- Opposite: Oppression

Hoham, king of Hebron

- Meaning: Whom Jehovah impels
- Opposite: Religion

Piram, king of Jarmuth

- Meaning: To bear fruit
- Opposite: Poverty

Japhia, king of Lachish

- Meaning: May God enlighten you
- Opposite: Deception or blindness

Debir, king of Eglon

- Meaning: Speaker
- Opposite: Accusation

The plot thickened with this new information and some new understanding, but I did not yet have the complete picture. *Is this for me or for someone else?* I wondered. *Or is it something I'm supposed to teach?* I didn't know if I wanted it to be for me. As it turned out, it was. Apparently, I needed some light shined on my soul.

The Holy Spirit very much enjoys lovingly identifying, tearing down, and reconstructing the framework of beliefs that were not established by Him. When the Holy Spirit attacked my faulty grid and revealed my warped thinking, it was not to change me into something new. He had already done that two thousand years ago. Instead, He wanted to help me see myself the way He had created and then reconciled me to be—perfect and whole. I grow in this discovery as I see more and more what He has done for me. This was the beginning of that journey.

When I became aware that I may have been deceived far more than I knew, I became adamant about getting free—at any cost. My reputation and ministry were the least of my concerns. I had to get the truth into every area of my soul. The Holy Spirit blasted me with His giant searchlight and uncovered a multitude of things to which I had been blinded. He kicked out so many pillars that were not of Him, pillars upon which I had unknowingly become dependent. The process was simultaneously weird and fearful.

I saw a vision of myself as a circular object held up by a central support beam or pillar in the middle, which was wide and sturdy. Around the outer edges were a multitude of smaller, narrower beams. He told me the outer beams were delusions and lies I had allowed to stay in my life and that they were holding me up without me even realizing it. They were false comfort zones and control mechanisms caused by fear, lies and bad teaching. Those pillars were clearly within my control, and I was holding myself up by my own self-reliance. The weirdest part of all was that, until then, I had no idea they were there. It was time for them to go!

Then I saw Him kicking the pillars of bad beliefs out from under me in a lovingly aggressive manor, sweeping through with no relenting. How strange to have so many things revealed to me all at once and receive new revelation that contradicted the lies I had held onto for so long. How humbling to discover I had lived with unknown agendas in my life and relationships with other people. It hurt. But more than anything, I wanted the garbage gone. So I faced reality.

Nakedness before the Lord could seem like a terrifying and vulnerable position, but it was the complete opposite. I was forced to find out who I was and what I really believed in. When that kind of light is shined into your soul, you find out real quickly whether you believe in your beliefs or in Jesus, whether you have faith in faith or faith in Jesus. And amazingly, the more these pillars I had held on to for so long were removed, the safer and more whole I felt. Never once was I in jeopardy of falling.

When I explained to Shannon everything God was doing in my heart, she asked whether I was doubting or questioning God. It was a fair question. When people go through this sort of upheaval, if their faith is in their beliefs rather than in Jesus, it leaves them with a lot of very confusing questions. My experience was completely different.

In answer to Shannon's question, I shouted, "NO! He is the only thing that is real to me." And I really meant it. There is something so comforting and assuring in knowing that when everything is stripped away, Jesus is more real than ever before. Knowing Him was all that mattered to me; nothing could ever challenge that.

Here's how it went down.

The Hope of Glory

For several months, the Lord had been telling me two things very clearly: "Learn the gospel," and, "Open your eyes." He would say them over and over, but I didn't really know what He meant. I thought I knew the gospel, and I

130

thought my eyes were pretty open. Little did I know that my world would soon be turned upside down again.

"Of course I know the gospel, God," I would tell Him. "Here, let me preach it to You to prove I know it: Jesus, the one and only Son of God the Father, came to earth, incarnate, was born of a virgin, fully God and fully man. He walked the earth and grew in wisdom and favor. Even enduring temptation, He never sinned, walking in perfection and perfectly doing what no man could ever do. He fulfilled the law. He was crucified, died, and on the third day rose from the dead. He then appeared, doing cool Jesus tricks like walking through walls and hanging out with His friends for forty days before ascending into Heaven and sitting down at the right hand of the Father, where He continues to be the high priest on humanity's behalf. There. See, God. I know it."

"Sort of," He would respond. "That is what happened, but what happened?"

This was a very humbling thing to hear from God. But what He had for me, the revelation just over the crest of the next hill, would tie all my learnings together, crystallizing it all into a proper perspective for everything I had experienced on my journey. And of course, I would much rather His gentle correction to the alternative—ignoring Him and pridefully continuing in an understanding that limits Him. Though it is humbling, I am so glad the Holy Spirit reveals to me where I am wrong and enables me to humbly admit it so I can be led into the truth. We can all benefit from realizing we're on a journey of discovery led by the very one we're discovering.

And so it began, a revelation of the fullness of the one true God and His inhabitation of me. When I started to be awakened to the reality and ramifications of this wildly mystical union, He began to shred strongholds I had believed, allowed and encouraged. It all came to a head with Colossians 1:27. There, Paul clearly stated the mystery of all of the ages, hidden until the appointed time, which is *"Christ in you, the hope of glory."* God had done it again. He had done the unexpected and completely bypassed all human reasoning and logic. Very few understood what had occurred on the cross, but Jesus had explained to the disciples beforehand. He told them God would, for the first time, *inhabit human vessels.*

If you really consider it, it is quite an odd thought. It is like He is a body snatcher, possessing human bodies. That may seem silly, but it is really far more profound and mystical than anything we know. Just as Jesus was inhabited by the life of the Father as He walked the earth, now we too have this divine life *within* us.

This great mystery and revelation of God inhabiting His people was the crux of the apostle Paul's calling and message, which was about the fullness of time and the ministry of reconciliation. This revelation he did not receive from another person but directly from the Holy Spirit, who revealed Jesus Christ to him (see Ephesians 3:3; Galatians 1:12). I believe the revelation Paul saw was so profound that human words and language couldn't get close to conveying it. He was brilliant, yet he eloquently stumbled through trying to accurately convey the ramifications of the gospel.

Considering that the apostle John said all the books on earth couldn't contain everything Jesus did in His earthly ministry (see John 21:25), it is absolutely absurd to think the glory of His resurrection and our union with Him could be fully explained in the Scriptures. Only the Spirit of wisdom and revelation can illuminate our minds to the vastness of this mystery. A lot of people find this reality kind of scary because it seems to leave the door open for wild new doctrines that contradict Christ. While that may be true (and I pray it never happens), I refuse to allow fear of what might happen to keep me from pursuing the depths of the mystery of Christ.

As I studied the Scriptures, I found that Paul used a lot of space in his letters to harp on the fact that people were having trouble grasping freedom from the law. For this reason, he had to constantly go back and re-teach the basics of grace. It must have been frustrating for Paul to live in this revelation of goodness so profound it listed ecstasy as a side effect and yet, from this exalted and thrilling position, to need to address sexual sin with people over and over.

Paul's letters were written to people who, for the most part, couldn't maintain or manage the freedom he had preached to them. When I began to understand this, the message popped out at me in an entirely new context. I realized I needed to understand the revelation Paul understood. I needed to let it become my reality and to live from it. When I did, it would mean that much of what Paul wrote to the various churches, even though the concepts were appropriate and absolutely true to their various situations, would not necessarily apply to me. What he wrote, he wrote to address particular circumstances among people who, for whatever reason, had become distracted and could not live out of the freedom which stood at the very heart of Paul's teaching. I realized I needed to live according to the message of grace and oneness Paul preached and intended for all believers to understand—not according to the things he had to address in his letters due to the people's lack of understanding. This is exactly what Paul meant when he wrote:

And I, brethren, could not speak to you as to spiritual men, but as to men of flesh, as to infants in Christ. 2 I gave you milk to drink, not solid food; for you were not yet able to receive it. Indeed, even now you are not yet able. (1 Corinthians 3:1–2).

So much in Paul's epistles is written as correction to people who didn't understand the gospel and acted out of spiritual immaturity. He wanted to give them meat, but he couldn't, so he gave them milk. Over and over again, he pointed out why he did not explain the depths of this mystery because of the people's inability to grasp it.

Unfortunately, like so many Christians, I had read Paul's instructions to these immature believers as though—if I could get the guidelines and follow them perfectly—they could make me mature. The truth I was discovering was, when we follow God into a position deeper than what Paul calls "the elementary principles" and step into the depths of our inheritance as children of God, then we are headed in the right direction. This is revelation. This is "meat," the goods that Paul so longed to teach and strove to communicate. This is why rules and guidelines aren't that helpful. When Paul wrote down rules and guidelines, they were biblical concessions to people who couldn't handle their freedom. They were a crutch for people who did not realize or live out their righteousness in faith but instead practiced sin and foolishness by faith.

As God was showing me this, He made it so clear I needed to move beyond all doubts and fears and hang ups. Only then would I be able to press on with the knowledge that my salvation is just the launching pad or the starting point for an abundant life. The person of Jesus is the doorway. As we step through, we are thrust into the intimate black hole of the heart of God and are spit out the other side into the indescribable riches of our inheritance. We then realize we have been born from above in Him, and Heaven is not on the other side of another death, awaiting our entry. It is now! Thus, we live from Heaven toward earth. God was so eager to spend eternity with us that He arranged a far better situation than we ever could have concocted. He found a way to open the depths of His heart, the depths of eternity to us right here and now. His justice is amazing; we get everything here and now, not what we deserve but what Jesus deserves.

This revelation rocked my world. Suddenly I saw how so many of us get stuck in the entryway and never press on into the fullness of our inheritance. Then we invite others to join us, preaching that "getting in" is the destination. Believing that Jesus is the Son of God, who died for the sins of the world, is important, but that belief is just the beginning, the entrance, the doorway into an eternal journey of discovery and adventure in knowing the depth of the love of the Father.

I can't imagine being married to Shannon for seven years and still wondering whether or not she really loved me or whether she even liked me. How sad it would be if I had to learn rules to follow in order keep her from being angry with me or changing her mind about how she feels about me. That would absolutely suck. Yet that is how I used to approach my relationship with the Father.

Entering the Rest

When I realized all of this, my biggest question was, "What do I do now?" What should I do now that I no longer believe so much of what I had been taught? How do I cope when the lens through which I viewed the world was permanently adjusted—not gradually, but abruptly and violently? What could I do now that I had realized my efforts are no longer necessary and they actually block the divine destiny at work in and around me? How could I respond when I had been hit so hard by revelation knowledge that, as I staggered backward from the force of the blow, instead of falling to the ground I fell into a new reality—a new realm that is nearly unexplainable in human language and reasoning? What could I do?

The answer was simple. All I needed to do was *quit!* As I entered His rest, this new life became my lens for seeing everything. And from it, the forward motion of my life began to flow. Once this new foundation settled into me deeply, I found I could begin to pull on and activate my inheritance as a son of God. I could literally be a manifestation of Christ to the world.

Rest is a pretty big deal. And it is sadly misunderstood. Here's the thing. As believers, if we don't rest, it is proof we don't understand who we are and what Christ did for us. It means we don't realize that rest is not something we do but something we enter into. It is a gift given by a wonderful Father who designed this life to be way better than we could have asked for.

Yes, we should respect the natural body's need for rest, but that's not exactly what I'm talking about. That is a temporary physical rest, and though it is important, it is not the fullness of rest Christ has offered us. In Hebrews 4, I found an explanation of the goodness of the rest that has been gifted to us by Christ:

> *For we who have believed enter that rest, just as He has said, "As I swore in My wrath, they shall not enter My rest," although His works were finished from the foundation of the world. For He has said somewhere concerning the seventh day: "And God rested on the seventh day from all His works."...For the one who has entered His rest has himself also rested from his works, as God did from His. Therefore let us be diligent to enter that rest, so that no one will fall, through following the same example of disobedience* (Hebrews 4:3–4, 10–11).

According to Hebrews, after Jesus accomplished everything on the cross, He sat down at the right hand of the Father in a state of rest. He still sits there today, confident in the complete work He already accomplished. A lack of rest is the opposite; it is unbelief. When believers are stressed out and overwhelmed, they are not acting in their identity or in faith in Christ's finished work. For a believer, stress is not ever a natural reaction to crazy circumstances; it is a function of unbelief. In this way, rest isn't about doing or not doing; it is about what He already did!

This was mindboggling to me at first. How could I possibly accept such a blanket statement about life? Here's what Holy Spirit showed me. Jesus can relate to our struggles. He became flesh and struggled so we *do not have to.* When we feel lost and broken, He is there, and He desperately wants to reveal to us our wholeness, which He paid for, and renew our depraved thought processes in order to show us who He is for us and who He has freed us to be. He wants to show us what's possible. And that's exactly what He did for me. He showed me I can *actually* live in the reality of Romans 5:17:

> *For if by the transgression of the one, death reigned through the one,* **much more those who receive the abundance of grace and of the gift of righteousness will reign in life** *through the One, Jesus Christ.*

That is just incredible. Because of Christ in me, I can reign in life! I began to realize that all my ideas about wanting to be "real" with unbelievers and not come across as a know-it-all, though they sounded like wisdom to me, were not rooted in the all-sufficiency of Christ's death and resurrection and my destiny as an overcomer who lives from a place of victory. There is nothing more depressing than Christians who don't know who they are. That was me for so many years. The truth is, I am a new creation. Whether I feel like it or not, the truth never changes. My old nature died on the cross with Christ and was raised with

Him. It is no longer I who lives, but Christ lives in me. The only person I should relate to is Christ, the firstborn of many brethren. He is the one who lives in and operates through me.

Sadly, in many Christian circles, it is more acceptable to confess brokenness and sinfulness (that has already been done away with on the cross) than to confess the victory of Christ and the wholeness and new nature we inherited through Him. This should not be.

Reflecting on all this, I asked God, "Why is it so hard to believe the fullness of the new nature, our REAL nature? Is it because we can't see it with the natural eye or feel it all the time?"

He showed me that our inability to see does not make the truth any less true. In fact, Jesus clearly explained this is how the Kingdom of God works—believe and *then* you will see the Kingdom of God. In other words, our feelings and experiences can be deceiving. Instead, we must rely on what we know and believe because of what we have read in Scripture and heard God speak; that is what we live by. Faith comes by hearing, and hearing comes by the word of God. What an "aha!" moment!

No longer did I need to see myself according to the grid of Romans 7 (which so many preach as the believer's current reality). That's not me Paul was describing. And it wasn't himself, either, at least not his believing self. He was describing what it was like to live under the law, apart from grace. To sum it up, it was not much fun and brutally frustrating:

> *For what I am doing, I do not understand; for I am not practicing what I would like to do, but I am doing the very thing I hate. But if I do the very thing I do not want to do, I agree with the Law,*

confessing that the Law is good (Romans 7:15–16).

Thank God for Romans 8, where Paul shows the contrasting reality of a believer who is living according to the grace of God. What a relief it was to see myself in Romans 8 and to know I am truly free from the law of sin and death and, instead, living by the Spirit. I live in fullness and victory. And that is what the world wants. Never once, in my years of religion, did an unbeliever say to me, "How do I get this Jesus who causes you to be so normal, stressed out, and depressed? I have to have what you have!"

Of course not. But when I am under pressure and in the midst of craziness, and I still ooze peace and joy and have enough leftover to encourage others, love them, and even help them complete the work they are too stressed and overwhelmed to finish—*then* they want what I have. See, I am not giving them me; rather, Christ is loving them through me. He is the one they long to have. This is the reality of the Christian life.

Paul described this so clearly:

And do not be conformed to this world, but be transformed by the renewing of your mind, so that you may prove what the will of God is, that which is good and acceptable and perfect (Romans 12:2).

For who has known the mind of the Lord, that he will instruct Him? But we have the mind of Christ (1 Corinthians 2:16).

Prior to salvation, I was at enmity with God in my mind. That was my past reality. When I entered relationship with God through Christ, that reality changed. However, I didn't realize it, and I continued to oppose, in my mind, the truth of my identity in Him. When my eyes were finally opened to who I am because of what He did for me, I understood that He has settled my account. Therefore, I renew my mind regularly to the reality that I now have the mind of Christ and am indeed one with Him.

What a shift! To say I was reeling would be an understatement.

Chapter 11

Overhauled by Oneness

But the one who joins himself to the Lord
is one spirit with Him. —1 Corinthians 6:17

In the next phase of revelation, the Holy Spirit showed me I had inadvertently segmented my existence in Christ. Because I believed there were two natures, I saw the world and all that was in it through that lens. Because I lived as if I was halfway fixed up (half spiritual and half carnal), I had lots of add-ons—holiness, faith, peace, power, healing, prophecy, the gospel, you name it. They were all floating around my semi-identity in Christ.

When the revelation of the finished work of Christ and my unending union with Him became my one and only reality, I realized that is, in fact, the one and only revelation. There is no greater revelation of other things. He is the revelation, and the understanding of our union is all there is. Out of that flowed everything else; holiness, faith, peace, power, healing, prophecy, the gospel—it was all a part of Him.

Beforehand, I would have adamantly denied that I had segmented and compartmentalized my life in such a way, but I was deceived. In fact, apart from the revelation of the perfect completion of all work by Christ on the cross and our inclusion in the death, burial, resurrection, and now rest of Christ, I see no possible way to avoid living with superfluous, unbelief-based add-ons to the fullness and completeness of what He did.

When I really began to get to know the heart of the Father and receive the love He so freely poured out upon me, I would get so full of Him that I could barely stand it. This wasn't an emotional response; it was a mystical reality of my union and proximity to His heart.

The more full I would get, the more I would long to give some back to Him, because in His fullness, I needed nothing else. All of the issues and questions I once wanted to address with Him had disappeared, and all I could say was, "Glory" and "Holy." I had no words to describe the ecstasy I was encountering. I no longer felt only attached to my physical reality, but Heaven also became tangible, and my unity and oneness with Christ became more real to me than the natural realm.

Prior to experiencing this, I would have thought only one reality could be real at a time. That simply isn't true. The Holy Spirit was leading me into the realization of my fullness in Christ because of what He had completed on the cross. The fact is that not only am I currently seated in heavenly places with Christ—enjoying the love and affection between the Father and Jesus—but also the fullness of the Godhead dwells in my very being. This is very hard to comprehend in the natural mind, but it was becoming very real to me as I rested in the pleasure of His reality.

We can experience both realities simultaneously. It's not one or the other. Being filled with the Holy Spirit does not make you less able to be of earthly good. In fact, it makes you far more effective, because you are no longer drawing from your own abilities and power to accomplish whatever you are doing. His life flows through us, His thoughts become our thoughts, and we see everything through His eyes. His reality and our reality become one reality. It's only a matter of renewing the mind.

This revelation began to change everything about me— my thoughts, my actions and my intentions. I realized He really did accomplish everything on the cross, and I really did get to freely enter into the blessings and fullness of life in Christ. I realized my old sinful nature really had been nailed to the cross with Christ and circumcised away, once and for all. I realized the righteousness, justification and holiness I could not obtain by any work of my own had been given to me already as a gift through Christ. I realized Christ became the process on my behalf so I could enjoy Him and live out a life of fullness of joy. I no longer needed anything, because God withholds nothing from me. Everything had changed. I approached Him with the boldness of a son who has access to an inheritance greater than anything I can comprehend.

In these moments, I found myself wanting to give something back to God, because I was beginning to understand that He had already made provision for all my needs, beyond what I could even think or ask.

This became my question, over and over. "Lord, tell me about Your heart. What is important to You today? What are You excited about today? What are Your emotions? What are Your thoughts? What are You looking at? Where are You at work? How do You feel today?" And the crazy thing is He began to answer me, because He knew I really wanted to know and understand His heart.

Even as I type this, I have the most profound emotion beyond words, deep in my spirit. Not knowing the cause, I asked the Holy Spirit, "What am I feeling and why?"

He reminded me that I had asked Him this morning what He was feeling, and, rather than telling me today by His voice or by a vision, as He often does, He was letting me feel what He feels (I assume just a measure of it). The best way I can describe it is a deep, deep, deep desire and longing for intimacy—not out of need but out of desire.

In Everything

One aspect of the mystical union is God's presence in everything. When I first began to experience the presence of God, I became addicted to Him. I had to have Him as much as possible. The only time I could find to be alone with Him was 4 a.m., before our son would wake up, but that was not a problem for me. I would get up earlier than early to talk to Him, and He would talk to me. It was so much fun! I could hardly believe He was so real and so accessible. It wasn't just about the voice of God but His presence in everything—everywhere—and especially inside me.

Then, in the process of my second awakening, God gently revealed to me that I had unintentionally snuffed Him out of the majority of my life. I did this without even knowing, due to lack of understanding and agreement with bad teaching. Even though I was really good at being in His presence from 4 to 7 a.m. and during occasional walks or drives, I had segregated out life as spiritual and non-spiritual, and I only looked for Him in the spiritual half.

Now I see Him in everything. He is all in all. He is everywhere. He is in every situation. He is undeniably intertwined with all of creation, He is in everything, *and* all things are in Him! His presence is everywhere all the time, not just when I work myself up into a tizzy to realize it. I do not need to escape or get away to sense Him. He is in the mundane. He is in the diaper changing, in the paper work, in the Internet search. He is in the paperwork, in the drive, in the conversation, in the thought life. Every atom, particle, molecule, and cell is impregnated with His presence. He is what holds the universe together. He is inexplicably woven throughout all of creation. And all of creation is in Him.

God is more than a voice, more than theology or doctrine, more than an experience, more than a power. He is more than a savior, more than a healer, more than a deliverer, and more than a provider. He is even more than a creator. This is what the Bible says about Him: He is *"one God and Father of all, who is over all and through all and in all"* (Ephesians 4:6), and *"For from Him and through Him and to Him are all things"* (Romans 11:36). Yet somehow His fullness inhabits my very being. This reality is too amazing and mind-blowing for words. And humbling, too.

He allowed me to see I was unintentionally using Him for His voice, power, visions, and so forth. I didn't even mean to. So I asked Him if we could start over and if He could teach me how to love Him. He is so special and wonderful. My heart is so full, yet empty of foolishness at the same time. So we started over. This is how it happened.

Early one morning, I sat and pondered how far I had come and how helpless and out of control I felt without rituals and experiences to validate me. I knew He was in those things and had used them in spite of my lack of understanding, but He was saying it was time to give up so we could start over with a fresh foundation.

So I asked Him if we could do just that, start fresh. If He would teach me how to love Him for Him, not just for what He does and what He gives. As I spoke, my senses began to get almost numb, and I could sense something weird but cool was happening. All of a sudden, nothing at all made sense. I couldn't put together a logical thought; my cognitive faculties felt suspended, yet heightened, at the same time. My reality in Him was the only real thing to me. Everything around me was still there, but, to me in that moment, it almost didn't exist even though I was looking around and could clearly see objects. It was like God's unseen realm had flip-flopped with the natural realm, and, while my physical eyes could see the natural, I was perceiving everything through a pair of eyes that were not my own.

Eventually I was able to get unstuck from my chair and peacefully glide down the hall toward the bathroom. As I did, the only words I could say, over and over, were: "You are in everything." They were more than words though. A new understanding was being revealed to me, and my mind was being unveiled to the fact that Jesus really did reconcile the entire cosmos into Himself. Really and truly, nothing is separate from Him. The breaths of air I was drawing into my lungs contained Him; the hall I was walking in was a reality that existed within the Son. And I am inexplicably intertwined in Him. I am in Him, and He is in me.

In the dark, empty bathroom, with only minimal light peering through the window on the far wall, I looked into the mirror and directly into my own eyes. For years I had felt very uncomfortable doing just that. But as I gazed, I didn't see my own bluish green iris looking back at me; I saw the burning love of the Father locked on to me. I felt peace and warmth and a glowing, heart-melting fire. Remembering I had a 9:30 meeting, I reluctantly pried myself away and began my hour-long trek across the Causeway bridge.

Once in the car, I turned to the sports radio station and began to back up the car. The Holy Spirit said, "You can leave that on, and I will still talk to you, but wouldn't you enjoy the silence?"

Previously, I had often experienced really cool early morning God encounters, only to get in my car and head to work, letting everything fade away. But with the new revelation I had been growing in that morning, I knew something was different. I knew this wasn't going to fade out. Instead, I was going to stay in this state. This was my new normal.

So I turned off the radio and chose to just enjoy His presence, this fullness I was so privileged to experience. As I drove, I simply rested in the Lord. I chatted with Him and thanked Him for making it so dang easy. When I don't overcomplicate things and just rest in His finished work and realize my inclusion in the love of the Father, Son, and Holy Spirit, I am transformed.

By the time I was on the bridge, things began shifting again. I was behind the wheel of a car traveling at sixty-five miles per hour on a twenty-six-mile bridge. But as I began to get farther and farther enveloped in the presence of God, nothing mattered but what He was doing. Before long, I was in a full-on trance and was literally watching myself drive over the bridge, but I was not at all present. I still don't know how I managed to get over the bridge, but, as I drove, I was fully in control of the car and relaxed; my spirit just was not included. The entire way over the bridge, I talked to the Lord, listened to the Lord, and watched open visions in which the Lord demonstrated what it looked like to live in this state all the time—naturally. I was finally starting to understand what this journey across the bridge is really all about.

Relationship

Amazingly, I discovered God is deeply and primarily interested in engaging my heart in a relational way. He is so real, available, and accessible. And the more I saw of Him, the better He looked. Of course, He wasn't changing; my perspective was.

We had agreed to start over in our relationship so I could learn how to really love Him. I desired this with everything in me. At first, I worked to develop my own relationship with God. It was great, to an extent, but I got hung up on some things I didn't understand. I began to ask, "Who do I talk to? Is it the Father, Son, or Holy Spirit?"

As I did, the Holy Spirit helped me understand, in more than just theory, that He had pulled me into the fellowship between the Father, Son, and Spirit. *What?!* I began to see my inclusion in Jesus' relationship with the Father. The personal relationship He had formed with me was for the purpose of lovingly and relationally leading me into realizing and enjoying their relationship and my existence in the middle of it. Out of that perspective, an individual and unique relationship with the Father, Son, and Spirit is not only possible but beyond natural and free.

We know it to be true that all of Scripture (Old Testament and New) is about Jesus. The Old foreshadowed the coming of the Messiah—the Second Adam and Savior of the world. The New (after the gospels) points back to what He accomplished and the implications of it. That is absolutely, unequivocally true. The best part is that while all of that is about Jesus, He is all about me—and you! His obsession and all of His focus is on our ability to abide in His perfect communion with Himself.

He reconciled all things into Himself on the cross, and declared peace (see Colossians 1:19-20). His conclusion and belief about us is clearly expressed through Jesus loving sacrifice. It is finished and settled in His mind. We, however, once alienated and hostile in our minds, were unaware of our reconciliation through our inclusion in His death (See Colossians 1:21-22), and are in the process of discovering who He is and what that means for us. I don't invite Him to live in my life or world; He has pulled me into His life and world, and I ask Him to show me this.

Every day I tell Him I don't want my delusional, fragmented world of understanding. "I want Your world and Your perspective. Give me eyes to see and ears to hear."

From Sin to Intimacy

This revelation is the key to living a holy life.

Until God began this second awakening in my heart, I held the majority view on sin, which means I believed in a big devil. Like so many, I had greater faith in the power of sin than I did in the power of Jesus. I would not have said it that way, of course, but that's how I lived. The truth is, what Jesus, the second Adam, accomplished is much greater and more powerful than what the first Adam did. Simply put, Jesus defeated sin forever and then wooed us from the inside until we realize who we are.

Sin aims to bump a person out of the peace and rest of communion with the Lord by introducing fear, anxiety, doubt, and so forth. Thus, sin is a function of unbelief— unbelief in the finished work of Jesus, who has told us to rest in Him. When I figured out that not even scary old sin could separate me from God and that, even in my moments of great temptation, He is there, I began to access the force or power of grace. Grace is more than just a positional reality; it is the actual power that enables us to not sin. In other words, I realized He is just as here, present with me in my moment of hiding, as He ever has been. Once I got that, I understood that I have no power in my own efforts to not sin. Instead, I drew upon the empowerment of His grace in order to yank me up out of the pit. What a relief it was to finally stop trying to do it on my own.

Here's the deal. He has already defeated whatever I may come up against, and the only thing I can do is take a deep breath and ask Him to take care of it for me. That's the reality for all believers.

Of course, we all know God hates sin, but we seem to forget He defeated it on the cross. We say out of one side of our mouths that we don't have to be cleaned up to come to Jesus, yet, out of the other side, we say He cannot look upon sin. So we end up living a life of slavery to sin. We say we believe in the grace of God, yet we disqualify ourselves in our minds from said grace because we are sinning, all the while not realizing grace is the actual force that drives us out of sin and empowers us not to sin. It essentially is the kryptonite to sin.

For a long time, I lived like I had to earn God's grace. Then God allowed me to see the reality of what I believed, and something forever shifted in me. I now feel the grace and presence of God more intensely when I sin. This triggers something so deep inside me that everything shifts. The awareness of anything but the love of Christ fades, and, all of a sudden, I find myself filled with distaste for that sin. This was such a pivotal paradigm shift for me, because before, I would try really hard not to sin. It was my own effort and my own power, and it was very hard and frustrating. Now, holy living is more than effortless. I am not just practicing prohibition of sinful activities; I am constantly growing in walking in the fullness of my identity.

The truth is, I live according to what I believe to be true about myself. That's true for all of us. If I believe I am a worthless sinner, I will act like and manifest the fruit of a worthless sinner. But if I believe the truth of the Bible— that I am a son, an heir, and a priest; that I am the righteousness of Christ, holy and sanctified—I will live out and manifest the fruit of the Spirit and release the fullness of the love, peace, and joy of Christ everywhere I go. It really is that simple.

When I am feeling anxious, fighting stress or fear, or am unable to rest or find the peace of Christ, I sit still and get quiet. As soon as I do that, I find quietness hard to come by because the noise of whatever lie or deception is vying for my attention gets very overwhelming and loud. At this point, rather than trying to fight the deception directly, I ask the Holy Spirit to identify the deception, lie, or deceit I have knowingly or unknowingly embraced. There is a thought process that has led me to attempt to live contrary to my identity in Christ. I somehow forgot that it is no longer I who live, but Christ who lives in me. Therefore, I humble myself and invite Him to shine His light on and through my soul in order to reveal any garbage hidden there.

Everything starts to change at this point, because, when I am deceived, I have no idea what I need. Identifying the problem is a big deal, and only He can do it for us. Not only does He identify the problem, but He is also the only one who can cleanse that particular area by washing it with truth. Renewing the mind is a fun, freeing, and intimately interactive event that—while it may look similar time and time again—is not a formula. It is taught and led by the Holy Spirit.

As my discovery deepened, I realized more and more that I am His expression on earth. In my work and my relationships with others, He operates through me. Through me, He relates to humanity, and I am a manifestation of Him. The more I understand there is absolutely no distance between Him and me, the more He flows through me. I don't need to do anything to get to Him, because I am in Him already, and He is in me. He is the one who came to this earth and embraced all of us into Himself. That means we have no chasm to cross; He crossed it for us. I have no existence apart from the Father, Son, and Spirit. We are eternally bound and inseparably linked, and the life I live is

His life lived through me. He comfortably wears my earth suit, and He is quite fond of it. I grow in understanding of this reality. It doesn't become more true as I realize it, it already was. The more I learn to humbly yield to His leading, and His will, the more evident this manifests in and through my life.

Now that is a revelation.

Chapter 12

Found in the River

He who believes in Me, as the Scripture said,
"From his innermost being will flow rivers of
living water." —John 7:38

One day, God told me, "Don't look at the horizon. Find the river." In other words, don't look outward; look inward.

Yes, we are called to be an outward manifestation of Christ on the earth. He wasn't contradicting that. What He was saying is that we don't become outward in nature by *trying* to be outward in nature. We are not called to stare off at the horizon, looking through our own eyes and trying to force opportunities or make things happen.

Instead, we seek the river of life. We dwell in the streams of living water, which flow from our innermost person, and the source of this river of life is the throne of Heaven. Then and only then will He point us outward and send us outward to love and serve and manifest Christ to the ends of the earth. Many of us get ahead of ourselves and fly off without the leading and direction of God. Or we hear from Him and quickly ride off according to some perceived direction and leave Him in the dust (metaphorically speaking). Of course, it is important to note that the inward focus is not a self-centered focus of selfishness; it is an inward Christ focus.

As God spoke this to me, I realized the Christian life is not about looking into the distance, trying to decipher where Jesus is, and then, once I recognize Him, trying to figure out how to get to Him. No, the person I live for lives in me. I am so one with Him that there is no me and Him, and that means *following* looks a little different than I thought it did before.

The love of God is not a spigot God turns on and off. He does not sit with His hand on the lever waiting for me to behave, follow the rules, do good stuff, or ask for it the right way. I do not have to say the magic word or utter the perfect prayer to appease a far off God before He will turn the nozzle and allow His love to flow my way. I am so glad that lie I once believed is just that—a lie. The truth is, He is the love I want, need, and desire; and I am eternally, inseparably intertwined with Him. His person is the love I so long for, and He is within me right now, in my very spirit!

Paul wrote about this in Ephesians 3:20: *"Now to Him who is able to do far more abundantly beyond all that we ask or think, according to the power that works within us."* The love at work for me and you, on our behalf, is at work from within us. It is the presence of His person within us. We don't look off into the distance for a love connection; we already have it. When we ask the Holy Spirit to open our eyes and give us the grace to comprehend what we have in Him, everything changes.

Expansion

One day when I was enjoying God's presence, I "phased out" into another place—not asleep but not awake. When I came to, my eyes were closed, and I could see myself from the inside of myself. I was down where the belly would be, but there were no internal organs, just a substance that I knew to be Spirit. It was traveling upward, and I was watching and traveling with it. I heard over and over again, "I'm expanding you. I'm expanding you. I'm expanding you." He was filling up my person with the awareness of Himself, and, in the process, He was searching and destroying any opposition to Him in the form of deception by renewing my mind. He told me this is done by revelation, revelation that brings understanding, wisdom, and knowledge of Him and who He is.

As I watched with my spiritual eyes, this presence expanded steadily closer to the outer shell of my person, and I wondered, *What happens when it goes past my skin and out of me?* I got my answer when it expanded straight through my skin. Before long, my inner man was significantly larger than my earth suit.

As this was happening, God explained to me that the understanding of this expansion is what we call spiritual growth. He said it is not just some abstract term that describes an accumulation of head knowledge; it is a knowing by revelation that becomes reality to us; though it is unseen by the natural eye, it is real nonetheless. In our inner person, if we walk in the Spirit and cooperate with Him, we are literally constantly growing larger as we develop in our understanding of who we are in Him. He said, "This is what many refer to as a 'greater anointing,' but it doesn't fall from Heaven. It flows and grows from within." It can only come by way of the Holy Spirit's illumination inside a person.

"Begging for it," He said, "is the most surefire way of not receiving it." It comes from the place of rest and communion with the Holy Spirit, as does everything else in Him. It cannot be obtained, because it is revelation of what is already within. As we grow in the revelation of Christ in us, we will walk in a bigger stature because our eyes will have been opened more and more to who He is in us. This is the renewing of the mind of Christ in a person. Through His faith, He opens our eyes to this reality.

All believers live with an understanding of Christ in them; it just varies greatly from person to person. He is real to all of us in a measure, and the measure increases as we allow Him to reveal this to us. He doesn't change; we do! This inner growth happens, and a change in the natural occurs in response to this inner change. Many times, ambitious people will promote themselves beyond where they have any business being because their eagerness to accomplish things outpaces their desire to grow in Christ. When this is true, bad things can happen.

After telling me these things, the Holy Spirit then told me to open my eyes. He has told me that many times for many reasons, but I never seemed to catch on to His point until well after the fact. This time was different, however, and I really can't say my response was my own. The immediacy of it and the ease with which it rolled off my tongue, with no pause for preparation, was evidence He had fed me the question and also provided the correct response, and I was a bystander in the form of a student.

Life somehow made sense in a whole new way as I boldly replied, "You open my eyes. I can't! I cannot do it on my own." Even if I could open the eyes of my heart, which I can't, I would not have been able to comprehend what He showed me. So I asked the Spirit of wisdom and revelation to unveil and open my eyes so I could see.

Revelation knowledge is astounding. What should take months or even years to understand is downloaded into the deepest parts of my being in an instant. (And this isn't just for me but for all believers.) There are many occasions, for example, when I realized that I knew things about God or particular Scriptures that I had no memory of learning and didn't even realize I knew. Like a spiritual download, I had learned it in an instant while communing with God outside of time and space, where the limitations of the natural realm become obsolete. In moments like these, I find comfort in knowing I am a part of something so preposterously large. It is so large I need grace just to believe it and not look at it as foolishness or say it is too good to be true. It is nice to be in the hands of such assurance as I leap into the river of His presence.

Two Cylinders

One beautiful day, as Shannon and I were driving through the beautiful historic streets of New Orleans, God gave me a vision that conveys so well the reality of looking inward to go outward. As we approached a stop light, it switched from yellow to red. Right as we halted, in the middle of the conversation, I saw a vision. It was a visual aid from the Lord to help me understand and articulate the idea I was attempting to express to Shannon.

Our conversation related to releasing the power of God. As I spoke, I saw two hollow cylinders or pipes. Each had a hole in the middle of the cylinders' sides; the hole was in the identical location on both cylinders. The Holy Spirit told me the two cylinders were described as separate. The first was me, and the second was Him. Then He put the cylinders together. One was inside the other, but the holes were not lined up. Inside the combined cylinders was an immensely powerful presence He described as His power. However, because the holes in the two cylinders were not aligned, the power was confined to the boundaries of the cylinders.

Then the cylinders began to turn until the holes were flush in alignment, and the power that had been harnessed within the two was able to blast through the aligned holes and emit a force that resembled a laser, a blinding force of loving power. In other words, as we come into alignment with Him in our thinking and faith, expectancy and belief take the place of doubt, fear, uncertainty, and self-consciousness. Then the power within us cannot be contained; it blasts the world around us with its transforming nature.

The Tunnel

The effect this revelation had on me looked something like the following vision the Lord gave me. I was walking down a long, dark tunnel with just enough light to give my immediate location context. I could make out, with the very limited visibility, that my setting appeared endless and empty. I was alone in this misty, dark, damp, and lonely prison, with no apparent hope of escape or glimmer of anything exciting.

It seemed all I could do was walk straight ahead. Backwards, for whatever reason, was not an option. Suddenly, I was startled by a brilliant light that appeared without warning from around a turn. The shine wasn't the yellow glow of an incandescent light bulb or the intensity of a halogen emission. This was the light of a thousand suns. The illumination allowed me to see that the tunnel was a subway train tunnel, and the source of the light was a train headed toward me at a blinding pace. I knew deep inside my soul that I had to get on that train. But how could I ever accomplish this when it traveled toward me with such speed? A second later, without time to think things through, I stretched my hand out and caught, by a handle I hadn't seen, the train I knew I needed to be on. I knew there was no possible way I could have reacted quickly enough, nor did I have the strength or agility on my own to grab and maintain a grip on this train. Yet there I was.

As the train rushed forward, I was able to fight the force of the oncoming wind and, through this superhuman empowerment, eventually reached the door of the car I had grabbed. *How did that happen?* I wondered. The door swung open, and I fell through, out of the chaos of emotional, mental, and physical blankness and into the train car filled with warm, dim, inviting light and cozy peace and joy that surpassed words. Still in the same tunnel, on the same track, moving at the same speed in this new direction, everything was different inside the train car. I felt safe. I felt at home.

As I sat in the train car, perspective began to shift, and I began to view the events that had unfolded. My vision zoomed out, giving me a different view and revealing that the tunnel was inside the heart of the Father. I was never separated; I was always in His bosom. He found me in my darkness and deception in order to show me I had already been found. I watched as I was grabbed onto the train and made my way to the door, seeing that it wasn't by my own effort. He came to me. He turned on the light. He grabbed me and pulled me out of my darkness. He then revealed to me His conclusion about me—that in His mind—it had been settled before the creation of the world (see Ephesians 1:3-6). I had already been reconciled to Him; I just didn't know it, and by faith, hadn't activated it.

Overflow

This union-with-Christ revelation began overwhelming me to the point of complete and utter helplessness apart from God. Without His life and power, I could do nothing. Meditating on this truth and His presence regularly caused me to become intoxicated by His glory. It was different than a drunken stupor. What I was experiencing was far better—a very clean and smooth feeling of exhilaration. In His presence I felt very relaxed, full of perfect peace, calm and collected.

The Holy Spirit really put this line of thinking on the front burner for me one evening when I was angered by something, and I could sense the anger filling up my body. It actually caused me to feel warm and even perspire a little bit. I asked the Lord, as this feeling arose in me, "Why is it so profoundly real and powerful in me?" Then it clicked. The sensation of negative feelings and emotions are often acceptable and normal to believers, but equating the presence of God with a feeling is somehow perceived as wrong or abnormal. The truth is, the reality of Him in us should be far more real to us in every way, even in physical manifestation.

That does not mean we are led by our feelings. I never evaluate my closeness and rightness with God by whether or not I tangibly feel Him. However, I do think I should feel Him more tangibly, more often, and more strongly than I feel negative emotions like fear, doubt, anger, and lust. The wrong way to approach this is to believe that if I sense Him physically, then I am closer to Him or more spiritual. The opposite is true: I sense and feel Him most when I understand I cannot get any more right or close to Him.

In my life, this wonderful sensation of God's presence went from rarely happening to becoming a daily occurrence to happening almost all the time. It was incredible! The source of the manifestation, of course, is Christ and the realization that no real separation exists between me and Him. Experiencing so much of His fullness had made me hungry to share that experience with others. I wanted them to have just as much fun as I was. So I began asking the Lord for the words to clearly express and communicate this revelation to people. I knew, apart from the Holy Spirit opening their eyes in the process, my words were meaningless and could even be damaging.

As the days went on, I began to have people come by my office to visit me and meet with me. The first one was a very dear and wonderful man. He is profoundly gifted and has a beautiful heart. We really didn't know each other, but we had met a few times—all of which were supernatural set-ups. When he entered my office that day, neither one of us knew the purpose of our meeting. There was no agenda on either side of the desk. All we knew was that the most recent of our interactions had been the day prior via text message.

That afternoon, I had gone for a walk around the Bayou to talk with God, as I often do, and the Lord mentioned this man out of the blue. Because I hardly knew him and hadn't seen him in awhile, I told the Lord, if He wanted us to get together, He should have him contact me, and I would be readily available. When I got back to my house, I discovered a text from this friend.

Our divine run-in prior to that happened this way. I had met a friend for coffee, and after the meeting, the Holy Spirit told me to go for a walk. As I casually strolled along the sidewalk that edged the busy street, not knowing my purpose, I heard a car horn and someone yell my name. I whirled around to see this same man, who at that point I had only met once before. When I walked up to his car and greeted him, he told me he had been driving the other direction when He felt like he was supposed to turn his car around. As soon as he did, he saw me strolling down the sidewalk.

Prior to that, at our first meeting, I saw him at a church service, and the Lord gave me some very specific insight about this man whom I had never met or seen before. It was intense but wonderful to be able to deliver a word from the Lord to this man about how gifted he is and how God intends to grow and use his gift.

That's the story leading up to this meeting in my office. We both were aware God was up to something we really didn't understand, and we knew we were exactly where we were supposed to be at that very moment. A fantastic conversation ensued. I wasn't planning on doing much talking, but for some reason, he asked some amazing questions that seamlessly made way for me to share with him the revelation the Lord had been teaching me. His questions then transitioned into the topic of hearing God and relating with Him, among other things. His questions were brilliant, thoughtful, and very refreshing. I was so encouraged to hear these kinds of questions coming from another person. I really don't have words to describe what ensued, but, as we trekked deeper and deeper into conversation about Jesus, we both became increasingly engulfed in the awareness of the glory of God in our midst.

In times past, when discussing things of God, I had done so anxiously and with vigor. I meant well, but the way I handled it did not minister life. This time was different. I had invited the Holy Spirit into all of it without effort by discussing the fact that He is in all and through all and that He is everywhere, including in me and in my friend. What I didn't do was pray, strive for, or beg the Lord to show up. He just liked the fact that I had eliminated every known barrier that would barricade Him from us in our minds, and, before we knew it, we were completely blasted—completely overwhelmed by His presence.

My friend said, "I feel like I'm in a bubble."

I was so thankful he said so, because I had been feeling the same exact thing, but, for fear of freaking him out, I had just rested in it without speaking of it. Once we acknowledged the presence of God, we became increasingly aware of Him, which led to us becoming more and more intoxicated with His fullness. The conversation got sweeter and sweeter, and it was apparent we were not the only two in the room. Such a peace filled the room that we became at a loss for words.

"My hands are heavy and shaking," he said, trying to put words to his experience.

Neither one of us wanted it to end. I watched him try to work up the will to stand up and leave. He had to get back to work and had already stayed longer than he intended. When he stood, I could see he felt torn between walking out the door to his responsibilities and just sitting back down and soaking in this wonderful ecstasy of Jesus. I didn't want to get out of my chair, either. *Perhaps if we just rest here, the moment doesn't have to end,* I thought to myself.

"I have never had a conversation about God like that," he said. "You talked about God, but didn't shove Him down my throat. You just gave Him to me"

"I just spoke a simple truth about who Christ is and what He did and who we are in all of it," I said. "And I invited Him into our time, and He became known in a way that is far beyond anything we can describe with words. I can talk about a Jesus who is real, or I can show you a Jesus who is real. We just had the pleasure of experiencing someone who can never be described in human language. But it wasn't my fault or the result of my efforts," I added. "I was just a spectator and got hit by His presence just like you."

I learned from his text messages over the following days that my friend had been rocked to the core by God, and it had nothing to do with me. He asked me, "What did you do to me?!?"

"Nothing!" I responded.

I didn't even remember until a few days later that I had been asking God for the words to explain this wonderful reality of which I had become aware. And He had answered in typical Holy Spirit fashion—not in the way I wanted or expected. Rather than giving me language—a formula—He started doing something so much better, something way more humbling and undeniable. He started bringing people to me, and, when they were around me, they would become intoxicated—not with me or anything I could say or do that was impressive but with the peace, rest, and joy of the Lord. All I did was get out of the way. He also gave me a great new friend.

The day after my meeting with this man, another good friend came in to see me as well. He only intended a thirty-minute stop, but thirty minutes became four hours and lunch. The same thing happened to him that had happened to my other friend. I watched as the wonderful bliss of Christ consumed and overwhelmed him. His eyes became increasingly glossy and glazed. Eventually, he couldn't speak. His hands became very heavy as he enjoyed this amazingly warm and fully unspeakable pleasure. The intensity and stress with which he had walked into my office completely fell away as Christ became more real to him than anything else in his world.

Chapter 13

This Is Your Story, Too

Truly, truly, I say to you, he who believes in Me,
the works that I do, he will do also; and greater
works than these he will do. —John 14:12

That's my story, the beginning of my journey on to the longest bridge across water, which is really the journey into the heart of God. No place is deeper or wider; we cannot travel its length. We can only begin an eternal journey of discovery of our oneness with the Father and His great love for us.

This is my story, but it's your story, too. Or, at least, it can be. Hopefully you can tell I'm not extraordinary, at least not more so than you are, or each of us is. Our Heavenly Father wants to do all this and more in you, too. He has already given it to you, through His accomplishments on the cross, and He wants to renew your mind and open your eyes so you can see.

I know this because He told me. I didn't write this book for me. I already know every detail. He asked me to share my testimony of awakening with you, because there is power on a testimony. He wanted me to tell you what is possible for you, too. To inspire you to enter into an exploration into the depth of mystery, that is His heart.

165

When Impossible Is Possible

Here's the key: believe in the impossible. I largely attribute the journey recorded in this book to my desire to see God move beyond what I understood of Him. He gave me faith to expect things of Him I had never seen. The way I see it, God is God, and He is infinitely larger than both my perspective and understanding of Him. Because I believe that, I make space for Him in my world. He is allowed to do whatever the heck He wants around me, even if it defies my understanding or even runs contrary to what I believe about Him. He has the right to offend my mind all day every day.

Some people might call that dangerous, but I am tired of natural wisdom. Too often, what seems wise to people is, in reality, nonsense. The fact is, God will *never* contradict Himself, and He gave us the wonderful gift of Scripture, which serves as a necessary tool to help us test what we hear to be sure it is in fact from God. However, that does not mean He is limited to the confines of Scripture. In other words, He won't contradict the truth of Scripture, but He might contradict our understanding of it. And He certainly will do things not previously done in Scripture (as long as they don't contradict His character as revealed in Scripture).

The days are over when we can sing about nothing being impossible while living lives very much confined by what is humanly possible. More and more, the belief that literally all things are possible through Christ, who strengthens us, is becoming far more real than any perceived impossibilities. I am simultaneously very much at rest and yet deeply burning to see this reality firmly rooted and bearing fruit in the lives of believers around the world.

I am not alone in this obsession. A company of impossibilities-defeating people is going to increase rapidly over the coming days. They are going to take Jesus at His word. They are going to believe He meant what He said when He said those who believe will do greater things than He did. These people will understand what they are packing—the Kingdom of Heaven—and, rather than begging for a move of God, they will know they *are* a move of God. When they show up, God shows up; and, when God shows up, the stuff happens.

We need to redefine the future as indefinable. When we do, Jesus will pull us into the impossible and indescribable; thus, He will define things for us. We will essentially begin to learn to take God out of our mental boxes (of course, He has never been and can never actually be in a box, but, in our perception, He was; that's what needs to shift). This shift in perspective is called learning to walk in the mind of Christ, first individually and, ultimately, corporately. If we preach anything other than a forward trajectory, heading into the great unknown of the endless extravagance of the heart of the Father, we are raising self-imposed barriers that will hinder our forward thrust.

Many people have already begun to be awakened and we are already well into the fun. Yet many in the Church are also fighting hard against the revelation of our identity in Christ and all that flows from it. The good news is, if you're reading this at a time when you feel like an outcast, you are not. You may just be a forerunner. Every day, I encounter more and more people who are so profoundly gifted and called by God but who are marginalized or unvalued by the Church. God hasn't forgotten them. In fact, God loves taking the unlikely ones and promoting them to be kings. Look at David. It is just His style.

Oh, the Possibilities

Together, I believe we're heading into something amazing. I believe we are on the cusp of an awakening of New Covenant Christianity, when large numbers of people will begin to know who they really are and live in the realities I've talked about in this book. The Old Covenant law-based systems will finally be seen for what they are, and the Bride of Christ will begin to live out of her oneness with and fullness in Christ. Oh, it will be glorious!

Envision a world of people who, empowered by love, *really* know nothing is impossible and continually push the boundaries of all known possibilities through Jesus. A people who know unbelief is the only barrier standing between them and impossibilities made possible. They will walk in the faith and expectancy that yield greater exploits than Jesus did. I see a movement of people who don't come together and complain about problems or make excuses for why they don't follow the Christian "rules" people say they should follow. Rather, when they come together, they can't wait to boast about what God has done and what they are learning, and they dream together about what's possible.

I see a people who know their Father is more than they could ever comprehend in a lifetime but are absolutely set on pressing into the things unseen and pushing collective humanity forward, deeper and deeper into what it means to be one with Him. They will be collectively obsessed with discovering the endless wealth, joy, and unspeakable treasures in Him. They will seek Him wholeheartedly, and He will guide them into all understanding and will teach them how He wants to relate to all of creation.

This is the people I see, the people about whom I dream. I will be one of their number. I hope you will, too.

The reality is, something incredible is stirring in the hearts of people all over the world. People's hearts and minds are being prepared for a mass awakening that began when the apostle Paul first received the revelation of the magnitude of Christ's death, burial, and resurrection. That revelation increased through the reformers and a multitude of revivals throughout history. Now it is about to explode into a whole new dimension!

God hasn't changed. He is the same yesterday, today, and forever. What is changing is our understanding of who He is; what He is really like; and how wonderful, loving, and for us He really is. This understanding is not extra-biblical; it is not new theology. It is a newly revealed understanding, from the Holy Spirit, of Paul's orthodox teaching throughout His letters. It has always been there; we just haven't fully understood it. The revelation was so good, so freeing, so powerful, so not about us and all about what Jesus did, that religion desperately desires to snuff it out. It says, "God can't be that good, can He?"

The answer arising from the Holy Spirit within His people is, "Yes, yes He can! And even better!"

This great awakening is already happening. All over the world, men and women are discovering *not* how to get closer to God but how close *they already are* to Him. They are discovering what He has already accomplished and given. People are sick and tired of the yoke of slavery, bondage, rules that have been placed upon them by fearful people who desire control. When they realize their freedom, they are so radically transformed and delivered instantly that they are free to love and to live by the law of the Spirit. Knowing their freedom from sin, they have no desire to sin, because they understand who they really are. This is becoming a reality in more and more people's lives as they say good-bye to religion and hello to the goodness of God. Change is inescapable. Resistance, by anyone or any force at all, is futile.

This new breed of people will be well studied, possessing a firm grasp of the doctrine and theology that has shifted their way of thinking. They will be a people of noble character. Their minds will have been renewed by the Word of God, and, therefore, accusations and doubt will not stick to them. And most amazing of all, this understanding will remove all self-effort and striving. Instead, they will live with full dependence upon Christ and the power of the Holy Spirit. They will truly know they are dead, and it is Christ who lives in them. They will not be tempted to take credit for the amazing things that happen at their hands, because they know it has nothing to do with them!

Thus, a Joe Shmoe accountant will produce more spiritual fruit naturally, with no striving, than some entire churches do. My point is, one man or woman who knows who he or she is in Christ can produce great fruit effortlessly. Imagine the impact of entire congregations walking in that reality!

Because Jesus is a person, not a franchise, this movement will take many different forms and expressions. The forerunners of this movement will be more concerned with establishing this understanding in people (with patience, love, and grace) and raising up other powerful men and women than they are with perfecting their strategy. They will value relationship with the Lord and other people over strategy. As this happens, everything will be about knowing Christ and Him crucified. People will walk in a new level of knowing Him, and, as they realize this, every bit of the focus they put on themselves will shift to Him as they, for perhaps the first time, understand they are worthy of being lavished with His love.

Here's the thing. Before you even believed in Him, He believed in you. He rigged the entire game on your behalf because of how obsessed He is with you. This train is moving, and it cannot and will not be stopped. Here's your invitation. Jump on board, and allow the Holy Spirit to free your mind. Learn to live freely and to love generously out of the abundance you have already received.

It is my joy to welcome you to the best life possible, the journey across the longest bridge, where impossibility bows to the unfathomable love and freedom in our Father's heart. I can promise you this: you will never be the same and you will never look back.

Made in the USA
San Bernardino, CA
19 October 2014